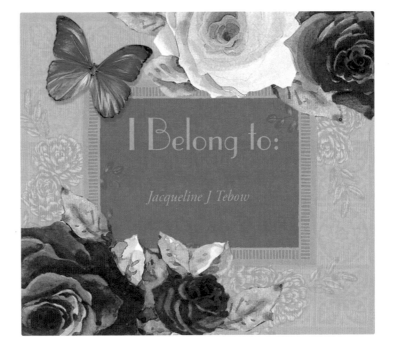

I Belong to:

Jacqueline J Tebow

—— A HISTORY TODAY BOOK ——

AGE OF CHIVALRY
Art and Society in
Late Medieval England

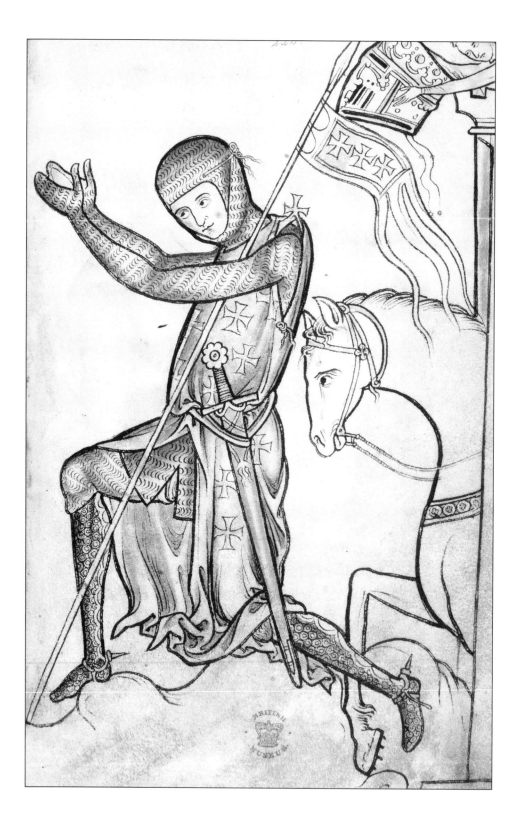

— A HISTORY TODAY BOOK —

AGE OF CHIVALRY

Art and Society in
Late Medieval England

Edited by Nigel Saul

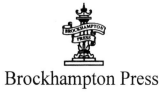

Brockhampton Press

Frontispiece: *The chivalric ideal: a knight dedicated to the service of God, from a Westminster psalter of c. 1250*

First published in Great Britain in 1992
by Collins & Brown Limited

This edition published 1995 by Brockhampton Press,
a member of Hodder Headline PLC.

ISBN 1 86019 146 0

British Library Cataloguing-in-Publication Data.
A catalogue record for this book
is available from the British Library.

Typeset by Bookworm Typesetting, Manchester
Reproduction by Scantrans, Singapore
Printed and bound in Great Britain by
BPC Hazell Books Ltd

CONTENTS

PREFACE

What was the 'Age of Chivalry'?

ONE OF THE MOST ATTRACTIVE DRAWINGS executed in England in the Middle Ages is that of the kneeling knight in the margin of a psalter in the British Library. Thought to be the work of an assistant of Matthew Paris, it captures perfectly the image of the Christian warrior. The young tiro is shown kneeling with his arms outstretched and his hands open. He is dressed in a mail hauberk, over which is draped a linen surcoat bearing the emblem of the cross patée. From his belt is slung a sword in a scabbard, and through his left arm passes a lance with a pennon attached. Behind him, leaning over the battlements of a tower, a page is caught in the act of handing down a tournament helm, while to one side a warhorse rises up and begins to canter forwards.

Deliberately, no doubt, the scene is conceived in a physical vacuum which gives it a dream-like quality. The knight appears suspended in mid-air. He turns away from, and not towards, the page handing down the helm. The warhorse is almost tripping over his left foot. Little or no relationship is established between the various elements that compose the drawing.

The effect of such licence is to present the knight in visionary terms: to invest him with hope and idealism, and to make him an image of human dedication. He is seen as no ordinary mortal, but as one of almost Christ-like perfection. Like Chaucer's Knight, he is 'a verray parfit gentil knyght', 'a worthy man', a lover of 'trouthe and honour'. Greed and avarice, and the other vices of which knights stood condemned, find no part in his nature. His ideals are the Christian ones of justice and truth, righteousness and peace. In his life he exemplifies all that was best in his order. In short he is the embodiment of the medieval chivalric ideal.

The ethic of chivalry had its origins in the military revolution which made the mounted knight the spearhead of medieval armies. It arose partly out of the camaraderie which developed between the young tiros as they trained and jousted, and partly out of the endeavours of the Church to moderate their violence and channel their energies towards ends of which it approved — in particular, the recovery of the Holy Land from the infidel. The basis of the cult was individualistic: what mattered were the brave deeds of brave men — through the performance of such deeds men gained in prowess and renown and won the approbation of their superiors and peers. With the passage of time, the glamour and showiness of the cult increased; tournaments developed into major social occasions, and the behaviour of the knights became more mannered and contrived. But all the while there was a serious edge to the proceedings which saved them from degenerating into exercises in escapism or frivolity. Only in the later fifteenth century, when the rise of standing armies undermined its individualist ethos, can chivalry be said in any meaningful sense to have 'declined'.

Given the importance of the chivalric ideal, it is not inappropriate that the major exhibition of 'Art in Plantagenet England, 1200–1400', held at the Royal Academy in the winter of 1987–8, should have been presented as a celebration of the 'Age of Chivalry'. Chivalry was not only a cohesive force among the European knightly class, it was also a major cultural influence in society. It inspired some of the finest writing of the period — for example, the troubadours' songs and the Arthurian romances. It also inspired some of the finest art — not only in a modest way with the drawing of the kneeling knight, but at a higher level with a work like the Wilton Diptych, which was in all probability a crusading icon. Architecture, the grandest art form in the Middle Ages, was not immune from its influence: castles like Warwick and Bodiam were conceived and designed purposely to give expression to its values, while churches like Etchingham in Sussex and St Mary's, Warwick, were rebuilt by members of the knightly class and bore witness to their values and self-perception.

To see the art of the late Middle Ages exclusively as chivalric art would, of course, be to misrepresent it. It was many other things as well. Above all it was Christian art. As often as not it was conceived in a Christian setting by artists who saw themselves as dedicating their labours to God. But to recognize this is not to reject the term 'chivalric art' as a tool of analysis. It still has its uses. It serves to remind us of the social and cultural influences on artistic creativity. It is the nature and character of those influences in the period 1200 to 1400 that are explored in the essays that follow.

Nigel Saul

I CULTURE AND SOCIETY IN THE AGE OF CHIVALRY

Nigel Saul

ARTISTICALLY, THE AGE OF CHIVALRY was the Age of Gothic — the age when European architecture was dominated by use of the pointed arch and the motifs derived from it. Advance and experimentation were its hallmarks. Masons (master masons were what we call architects today) broke new ground in the techniques and ideas that they used. They competed with one another in the size and splendour of their buildings. They tempted Providence in the heights to which they raised their vaults. Their achievements were some of the most prodigious in the history of Western art. Yet, curiously, at the time that the period opened they could hardly have been guessed at. Architecture was still dominated by the heaviness and solidity of Romanesque. It was only with the rebuilding of the abbey of St Denis, near Paris, in the 1140s that hints were given of the glories soon to come.

The abbey of St Denis was in a sense an unlikely place to give birth to a new style. The Capetian kingdom, in which it lay, was one of the least conspicuous of the many states that made up present-day France. Normandy to the north and Anjou to the west were far wealthier. Furthermore, it lacked a tradition of great church building: because resources were scarce, churches in the Paris region were small and undistinguished by comparison with those further north. But in a sense these disadvantages could be construed as strengths. The absence of received wisdom as to what a great church should look like left masons free to experiment: which is precisely what the master mason of St Denis did. Commissioned to remodel an eighth-century basilica which had a special place in the affections of the French kings, whose ancestors were buried there, he produced a design which was at once innovative and conservative. It was conservative in that it

Sens Cathedral, France, the interior looking east, c. 1142–76. Sens was one of the first cathedrals to be influenced by the new style of St Denis.

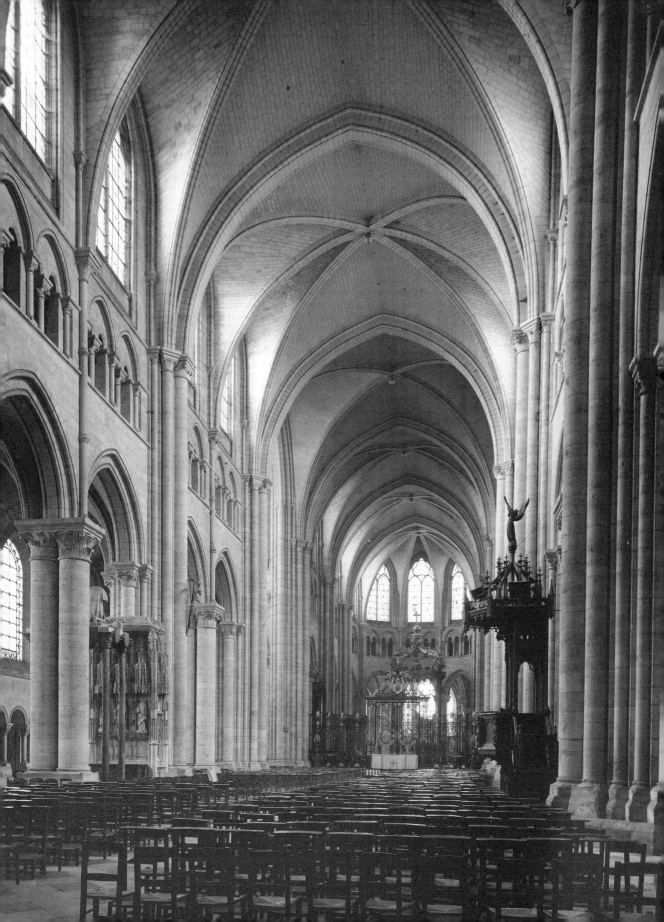

employed columnar piers like those of the eighth-century building — presumably to provide a measure of continuity; it was revolutionary in that it employed windows so greatly enlarged that seen from afar they seem to merge into one continuous band of fenestration. The idea was to flood the interior of the church with light — to banish the atmosphere of gloom that had enveloped the old Romanesque churches. The achievement of this aim was assisted by another Parisian speciality, and one that was carried further here than ever before — namely the systematic thinning-out of the wall structure. As in the church of St Martin des Champs, Paris, a few years earlier, a sense of spaciousness was created by eliminating the barriers between the various parts of the interior and reducing in thickness the wall separating the interior from the world outside. As a result, the building seemed to rise effortlessly in a way that only a few years before would have seemed inconceivable.

The importance of St Denis did not lie so much in the fact that it struck out in an entirely new direction, for it did not: many of the features that it incorporated had been employed piecemeal in a number of buildings before. Rather it lay in the novelty of bringing these features together with new consistency and clarity of purpose in a church which was bound to be noticed because of the royal patronage that it enjoyed. What St Denis did was to set new standards by which great church building could be judged — as the experience of the next half-century was to show.

One of the first buildings to bear witness to its influence was the cathedral of Sens in the south of the Île de France. The remodelling of the choir there had been initiated in about 1140 in a plain Romanesque style. But, when only the outer walls had been finished, the original designs were scrapped and a more systematically Gothic style was adopted. Window-size was increased; columnar piers were introduced (though this time coupled, and alternating with clustered piers); and the all-pervasive sense of bulk was discarded in favour of spatial openness and airy lightness. Also influenced by St Denis was the cathedral of Notre Dame, a few miles to the south in Paris itself. As at Sens, use was made of the now familiar repertoire of motifs — columnar piers, gently pointed arches and ornate foliate capitals. But a new look was given to the interior of the building by the strong accent on height, a feature which was to become characteristic of French Gothic in its maturity. From floor level to the apex of the vault was a distance of 102 feet, a height never before reached in a church. A positively ravine-like quality was given to the interior by the great cliffs of stone rising either side of the nave. Over the next half-century this sight inspired masons to compete with one another in the heights to which they raised their vaults. At Bourges in

Canterbury Cathedral, interior of the choir looking east, 1175–84. The gently pointed arches and acanthus leaf capitals bear witness to the French inspiration of the design (cf. Sens, page 9). The extreme length was needed to accommodate Becket's shrine; but an emphasis on length quickly became a characteristic of English Gothic.

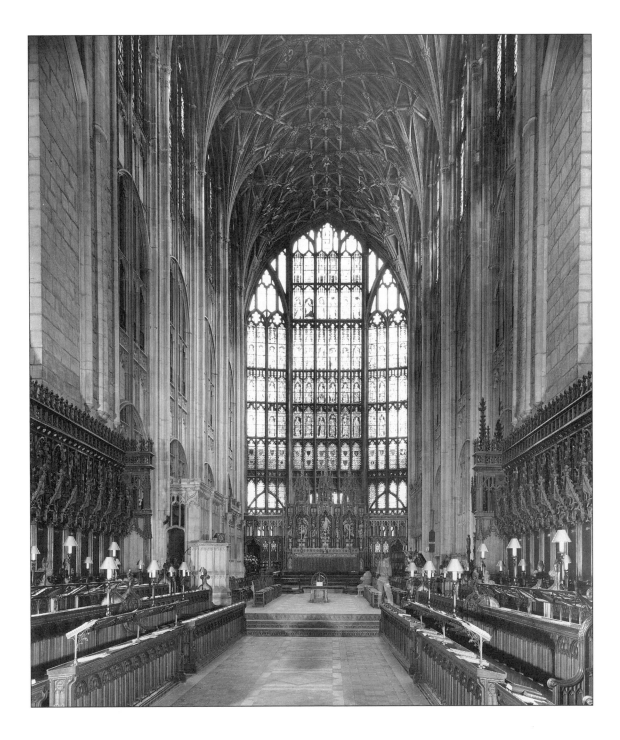

the 1190s they reached 120 feet, and at Amiens forty years later 140 feet. At Beauvais in the 1270s they finally went too far — with 159 feet. The vault fell in a few years after it was finished, and the piers had to be strengthened. Even in churches of lesser elevation built later, such as the abbey church of St Ouen, Rouen, a sense of tremendous verticality was imparted to the interior by the ruthless subordination of the longitudinal accent to the vertical.

In other parts of Europe, Gothic wore a rather different look. There was not such a single-minded pursuit of upwardness. Delight was shown in exploring some of the other possibilities in the new architectural vocabulary. In England, for example, there was an early liking for grand longitudinal vistas and for the elaboration of surface texture. Both characteristics are noticeable in a design of seminal significance for the development of Gothic in England, the otherwise largely French-inspired eastern arm of Canterbury Cathedral, begun in 1174. The large windows and columnar piers are derived, at several removes, from St Denis. The coupled piers of the Trinity Chapel and the triforium elevation of the choir are obviously indebted to Sens — which is hardly surprising since the architect was one William of Sens. But entirely English or Anglo-Norman in character was the long tunnel-like vista resulting from the need to accommodate the shrine of the recently martyred Becket and the delight in polychromatic effects attained by placing dark Purbeck marble shafts against the white stonework of the pillars and walls. Concessions of this sort had to be made to local taste to make the essential Frenchness of the design palatable to an English public.

The process of reinterpreting French ideas gathered pace in the next generation of building in England. Chichester and Lincoln, the cathedrals influenced most directly by Canterbury, showed further significant departures from mainstream Île de France Gothic. At Chichester the triforium of the new retrochoir was elaborated more than it would have been in France, and at Lincoln the tendency towards horizontality was stressed by the uncomfortably low springing of the vault. In the churches of the west of England, the influence of France was reduced still further. Such relatively major designs as Glastonbury, Abbey Dore and Worcester, all dating from the 1160s–1180s, owed little or nothing to Canterbury. They are products almost entirely of the Anglo-Romanesque tradition. At Worcester, in the western bays of the nave, Romanesque influence was particularly strong — witness, for example, the thick wall structure and round-headed arches of the triforium. Almost the only Gothic-looking element was the heavy use of shafts on the piers, though curiously even this had antecedents in the Romanesque — in the naves of Ely and Durham. Out of this odd assortment of motifs, however, a new synthesis was to be fashioned, one that took as its centre-piece the many-shafted, clustered pier. At Wells, in the nave and transepts rebuilt in the 1190s, it found realization. The complex patterning of the piers and the elaborate mouldings of the arches combined to produce vistas of unparalleled linear richness.

Within two decades of the arrival of full-dress Gothic in England, native masons were producing their own highly distinctive version of its idioms. Whether in so doing they may be said to have given birth to a national style of Gothic is, however, hard to say. 'National' styles were ill formed in the central Middle Ages. In France there was not one style, there were many. One flourished in the Île de France, another in Normandy, another again in Burgundy, and so on. It was much the same in England. One style took root in the north, evincing a preference for big east windows rising the full height of the building, and another in the south showing a preference for 'stepped' east ends with projecting lady chapels. Less distinctive traditions were associated with other regions of the country.

Despite the existence of these variations, however, a number of characteristics did emerge which were common to English Gothic as a whole. One was the fascination with length, which tended to give the interiors of English churches a tunnel-like quality not found elsewhere. A second was a taste for linear richness satisfied, as at Wells, by the multiplication of shafts and vaulting ribs. A third was the delight in surface texture which found expression in the creation of arcaded or panelled walls, elaborate triforia and rich sculptural adornment. These were characteristics exhibited most clearly in architecture, but they were also present in sculpture and painting. Linear richness was a hallmark of English illumination throughout the Middle Ages: it is seen in works of such different dates as the Lindisfarne Gospels (eighth century) and the Litlyngton Missal (c. 1383–4). Rich texturing of surfaces was equally popular in sculpture: this is shown by looking at works so superficially different in their treatment as the Ruthwell and Bewcastle crosses from the seventh century and the Kirkham Chantry at Paignton in Devon from the fifteenth.

The enduring presence of these characteristics is partly a comment on the conservatism of English taste. If a building was put up in stages, patrons wanted the later parts to bear some resemblance to the older. It was for this reason that Henry Yevele was required by the monks of Westminster in the 1370s to make the new nave harmonize as closely as possible with the choir of a hundred years earlier. A higher premium was placed on conformity than is often allowed. But purely aesthetic considerations were not the only ones involved. The English in the thirteenth century were a people rediscovering

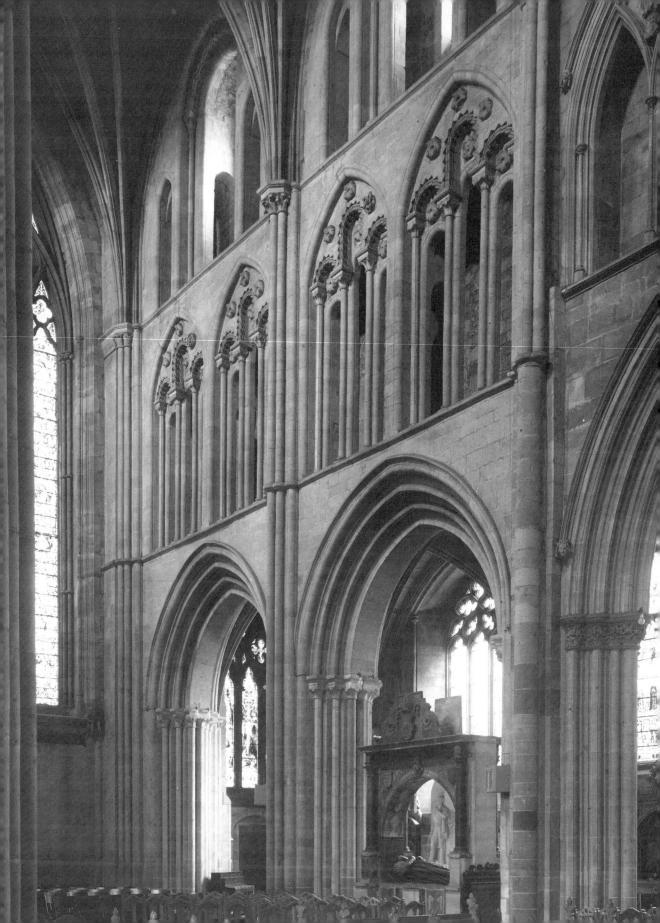

their sense of identity. The humiliations that they had suffered in the wake of the Conquest had all but passed. A sense of community was emerging which bound men together irrespective of race. The distinction that mattered by this date was not so much that between English and Norman as that between native and immigrant. With the Channel once more a boundary, the English felt themselves to be a race apart; they saw the French as their enemies, and the pope as a drain on their wealth. They considered their own traditions and customs the foundations of their strength: far better to nourish them, it was believed, than to seek inspiration from outside. Culturally, the effects of this outlook were felt in two ways. Firstly, a stimulus was given to interest in Old English art — Matthew Paris, for example, a skilled artist and illuminator, revived and developed the Old English technique of outline drawing. And secondly, there was a somewhat ambivalent response to the achievements of French high Gothic. While the sheer quality of the French work was recognized — its inspiration can be felt in such works as Henry III's Westminster Abbey — it was felt that it could not automatically be transplanted to England. Modifications were needed if it were to be assimilated to native traditions.

In the fourteenth century, the English aspiration to artistic independence grew stronger. The Perpendicular style of architecture, conceived in the 1330s and 1340s, though rooted in French motifs, became what has been called 'England's national style'. Its rigid rectilinearity, illustrated to perfection in the choir at Gloucester, stood in sharp contrast to the aptly named Flamboyant style of contemporary French Gothic. The style's rapid dissemination was probably a by-product of its association with the court at a time of English military success abroad. In 1340, Edward III had triumphed over the French fleet at Sluys. In 1346, he landed in France and defeated Philip VI at Crécy. Ten years later, his son Edward, the Black Prince, won another great victory at Poitiers and took the French king prisoner. The French monarchy was brought to the verge of collapse; in the event it survived, but its prestige was shattered for a generation. The English monarchy, by contrast, rose to new heights of glory. This was a reversal of fortune with important artistic as well as political consequences. Not only was a boost given to the spread of Perpendicular within England, encouragement was also given to the adoption of its motifs in Europe — even in areas like Bohemia which had hitherto looked chiefly to France for inspiration.

English military success in the mid-fourteenth century was not without implication for other areas of culture. Particularly important was the effect on chivalric romance. War and romance went together in the Middle Ages.

Worcester Cathedral, the western bays of the nave, c. 1175–80. An early response by masons in the west of England to the challenge of the architectural vocabulary.

Romance in a sense was an inevitable accompaniment to war: when the pain and suffering of conflict were so great, it provided an element of glamour which made the suffering seem worthwhile. The most astute rulers of the day were quick to realize this, and to cash in on it. Edward I, for example, in whipping up support for his wars, made the most of England's connection with King Arthur. In 1278 he was present at the reinterment at Glastonbury of the bodies of Arthur and his queen, Guinevere. In 1284 and 1302 he held 'round tables' at Nefyn and Falkirk respectively. And in 1306, on the occasion of the knighting of his eldest son, he laid on festivities which were said to have been unequalled in splendour since the coronation of King Arthur at Caerleon. Half a century later, his grandson Edward III exploited similar associations in the build-up to the Hundred Years War. He organized tournaments and round tables, and encouraged people to think of him as a second King Arthur. On one occasion, he even fought incognito in the best Arthurian manner. But in one respect his policy was altogether more inventive than his grandfather's. When he planned to establish an order of chivalry, he did not simply revive the Arthurian Order of the Round Table, he invented a wholly new one, the Order of the Garter. The origins of the Garter idea are obscure — almost certainly the story of the king picking up the Countess of Salisbury's garter and putting it round his knee is apocryphal; but the adoption of a *blue* device, with its allusion to the lilies of France, may suggest a connection with Edward's claim to the French Crown. The Order was established in the aftermath of the victory at Crécy, and its original members were leading commanders in the battle. Probably at one level the Order was intended to be a memorial to the victory. But at another it was almost certainly conceived as an instrument of policy — its purpose being to unite the great men of the day in honourable service to the king. They were to be bound in a relationship of equality with each other, but one of subordination and loyalty to the head. Arthurian models in this way were borrowed and turned to a new purpose.

The literary roots of this romancing were to be found in the so-called 'Matter of Britain' — that is, the cycle of tales concerning King Arthur and his knights. These tales were of Welsh origin, and were transmitted to the French-speaking world by Breton minstrels in the late eleventh and early twelfth centuries. By the likes of Wace, Chrétien de Troyes and Wolfram von Eschenbach, they were woven into tales of romance and love, fame and ambition. All over Europe noble audiences lapped them up. In the 1130s, England's Geoffrey of Monmouth gave a boost to the genre with his massive *History of the Kings of Britain* and *Prophecies of Merlin*. However, the great majority of English Arthurian romances of the thirteenth and fourteenth

Wells Cathedral, interior of the nave looking east, begun c. 1190. A mature example of the style evolved by the masons in the west of England. Note the strong horizontal emphasis and the preoccupation with linear richness.

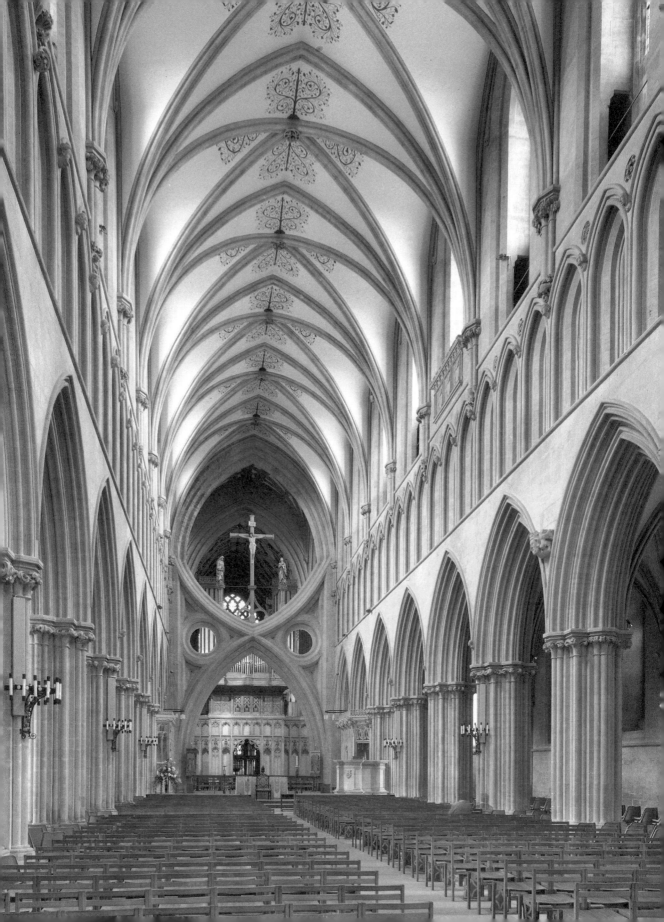

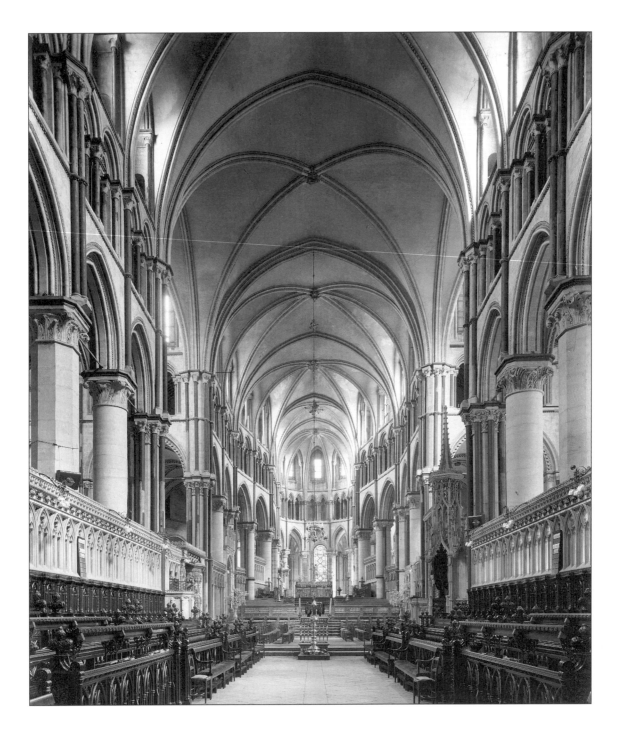

centuries were more heavily indebted to French than to English source material — and rarely distinguished themselves in the way that they treated either. This is the case, for example, with Lovelich's 'Merlin' and the stanzaic *Le Morte Arthur*. The one major exception is *Sir Gawain and the Green Knight*, written towards the end of the fourteenth century by someone from the north-west of England who had court connections. Though drawing like the other romances of the day on French models, it transforms them and invests them with greater significance. It is a poem unusually rich in nuances of word and mood. Yet, curiously, it never achieved wide circulation: it survives by the thread of a single manuscript. Of the many lesser poems composed at the time, a far greater number of copies are extant.

That there was a ready market for the literature of Arthurian romance there can be little doubt. It was the staple form of entertainment in knightly and baronial halls on both sides of the Channel. In the twelfth century, it would have been recited by minstrels. Later, lords would almost certainly have read it for themselves. Romances figure prominently in most of the surviving library catalogues of the period. Sir Simon Burley, Richard II's tutor and vice-chamberlain, had a 'book of romances of King Arthur' and 'a book of prophecies of Merlin'. Sir John Paston, a century later, had volumes containing the 'Death of King Arthur', the story of Sir Gawain and the Green Knight and an account of another mythical hero, Guy of Warwick. Reading — and in particular the reading of chivalric romances — was clearly becoming part of the nobility's everyday experience by the fourteenth century. So too for that matter was the commissioning of works of literature. Lords of all ranks gave encouragement to writers. Richard II urged John Gower to write the *Confessio Amantis*, and at about the same time an unknown lord in the north-west (Sir John Stanley?) spurred the Gawain poet to write the great poem from which he takes his name. The extension of patronage in this way served a number of ends. Most obviously it added to the corpus of literature to be enjoyed, but it also offered succour to dependants and legitimized aspirations to leadership in society. These broader considerations were of some importance to the working of lordship and 'bastard feudalism'. When, for example, the Gloucestershire lord, Sir Thomas de Berkeley of Berkeley Castle (d. 1417), commissioned from his chaplain John Trevisa translations of Higden's *Polychronicon* and Giles of Rome's *De Principe*, he was not only satisfying his own thirst for knowledge; he was also enhancing his repute at a time when he was being challenged in his domains by the rise of the favourites of Kind Richard II. To be seen to honour a writer could add greatly to a lord's prestige; it was part and parcel of the process of image-building.

Gloucester Cathedral, the choir: a Romanesque structure given a Gothic overlay, c. 1337– c. 1367. The fondness for panelled surfaces, so evident here, was a characteristic of English Gothic art.

Patronage, however, should not be seen as an exclusively male activity. If it sometimes appears as such, it is because men's activities are better documented than women's. Married women had no independent personality in law; any property they had passed automatically on marriage to their husbands. In terms of documentation, then, their own aspirations are concealed beneath their husbands'. Only in the case of those who either retained control of their property (that is, heiresses) or *regained* control of it (that is, widows) is the veil lifted and an insight given into the nature of female patronage.

What is immediately apparent is that both widows and heiresses alike accorded a high priority to expenditure on charity and education. Margaret, Countess of Norfolk (d. 1399), probably in response to the promptings of her confessor, spent sums on the repair of roads and bridges near her home. Katherine, Lady Berkeley (d. 1385), a lady twice widowed, in the year before her death founded a grammar school at Wotton-under-Edge which was to serve as a model for others of its kind. Lady Margaret Beaufort, mother of Henry VII and one of the richest women of her day, endowed professorships of divinity in both Oxford and Cambridge, and founded two colleges, Christ's and St John's, at Cambridge. The spur to this activity was to some extent provided by a concern for salvation: through the performance of good works on earth it was hoped to ease the soul's passage from purgatory to Heaven. But there was also a more selfless spirituality at work. Lady Margaret and her slightly older contemporary Cecily, Duchess of York, were in the forefront of the *devotio moderna*, the strong late medieval movement of lay piety. Both were unflagging in their daily routine of prayer. Cecily would rise at 7 a.m. and immediately recite matins with one of her chaplains. After breakfast she would go to chapel, probably in the company of her household, for the Office of the day and two low masses. Then, in the afternoon, having discharged her public duties and rested, she would devote what hours remained to reading, private prayer and contemplation. Lady Margaret — a friend of John Fisher and patron of the Carthusians — was equally rigorous in her devotions. She would rise as early as 5 a.m. and hear four or five masses before breakfast. In the remainder of the day, she would attend mass with her household and devote time to private reading and prayer.

Given the number of hours that these ladies spent reading, it is hardly surprising that they built up large collections of books. Cecily had copies of Walter Hilton's *Epistle on Mixed Life*, the *De Infantia Salvatoris*, the *Golden Legend*, a life of St Catherine of Siena and the Revelations of St Bridget. Lady Margaret had a collection which included a comprehensive range of devotional works, a number of which she had commissioned herself — for example, Wynkyn de Worde's edition of Hilton's *Ladder of Perfection*. To judge from the general character of these and other collections of the fifteenth century, it does not appear that female tastes had changed greatly over the years. Devotional works — in particular psalters and books of hours — had been popular with women since the beginning of the fourteenth century, if not earlier. Many of the finest manuscripts are thought to have been executed for women, among them the Queen Mary Psalter which, it is suggested, may have belonged to Queen Isabella, wife of Edward II. Women of high birth had the leisure to devote to such literature; and, provided they were not married, they also had the means to pay for it.

A necessary precondition for the success of a domestic regime like that of Cecily or Lady Margaret was the existence of a chapel in which mass could be celebrated. Before the thirteenth century, such chapels had generally been found only in the larger castles, such as the Tower of London. In the years that followed, however, they became more common. By the late Middle Ages, if not before, they had become a regular feature of almost every gentry manor-house. Generally they ran off the private apartments of the house. At Charney Bassett in Oxfordshire, for example, entry was gained directly from the solar — a space from which the later development of the withdrawing room developed. Since there was often no other interior access, an external staircase was sometimes provided to save the solar occupants from disturbance. With the passage of time, these domestic chapels became steadily larger and more elaborate. By the fifteenth century, they were equipped with statuary, fine plate, altar hangings, liturgical books and even relics. They were served by full-time chaplains or confessors; and, in the case of those with rich endowments, the services in them were led by choirs under the direction of a chapel master. They became the focus of the devotions of not only the lord and lady but their family and servants too. Through regular attendance at chapel, a way was found of bringing the household together in worship and of reaffirming the values which they shared as a community.

In the late Middle Ages there was an increasing need for such reaffirmation because of the breakdown of solidarity in so many areas of life. Proprietors were drawing ever more apart from their servants. They were abandoning the communal life of the hall in favour of the privacy of their chambers. The bonds which had tied them to their men were becoming more formal and less social. These were changes which were observed by contemporaries, and commented on disapprovingly. But there was little that could be done to stop them because they were part of a larger process of change in society. People were seeking greater separation from their fellows, not only in space but in rank. This was particularly noticeable at the top. The nobility were becoming separated from the gentry, and new ranks were appearing in both: in the nobility by 1500 there were those of duke, marquis, earl, viscount and baron, and in the gentry those of knight, esquire and gentleman. A similar process was occurring in the lower reaches of society. In place of the previously largely undifferentiated mass of landowners, there was now a carefully graduated hierarchy of degree.

Perhaps there is a likeness to be observed here with developments in art and architecture at the time. In the later phases of Gothic, there was a passion for breaking up and fragmenting space — on the continent even more so than in England. This is visible most clearly in the treatment of surfaces. Façades were covered by tier upon tier of panelling; aisles were enlivened by rows of blind arcading; vaults were turned into studies in linear patterning. Everywhere — on buttresses, canopies, towers — niche was piled upon niche to produce effects of unparalleled exuberance and complexity. A similar obsession can be observed in the way that piecemeal additions were made to churches. Rooflines were broken by the addition of towers, spires, turrets, porches and chapels. Vistas down naves were interrupted by screens, reredoses, statuary and a host of other fittings. Both within churches and without, unity was sacrificed on the altar of ceaseless elaboration. The result was a wholly different aesthetic from the chaste purity of early Gothic. Arguably it is the artistic equivalent of the process of division and differentiation observable in late medieval society at large.

To a degree, of course, the trend towards greater elaboration is explicable in terms of architecture's own immanent processes. By the mid-thirteenth century, the limits of technical possibility had been reached, and the urge to build bigger and better could only be satisfied by resort to further surface enrichment. However, there were also factors at work which suggest a link with the larger world. In the late Middle Ages, the main patrons of art were no longer the wealthy ecclesiastical corporations — the abbatial and cathedral chapters — for whom the great works of the late eleventh and twelfth centuries had been executed; by the fourteenth century, these bodies were having to keep a closer eye on their pennies. Instead, the initiative had passed to the host of noblemen, knights, esquires, burgesses and civil servants who, though collectively rich, were individually, with some exceptions, of lesser means. The result was a major shift in the direction of artistic activity. No longer did it focus as much as it had on the great abbeys and cathedrals — few individuals could afford to rebuild a cathedral from end to end. It now found outlet in the rebuilding or partial rebuilding of smaller churches, generally at parish level, and in the piecemeal embellishment of the greater ones. Favoured objects of expenditure were statues, tombs, chantry chapels, stained glass windows, alabasters and altarpieces. These were attractive because they combined flexibility of cost with opportunity for display; humble men as well as rich could afford them. Over the years, they multiplied in churches and cathedrals alike, filling the aisles, side chapels and other spaces. Obviously, there was a loss in the overall coherence of buildings. Late medieval interiors appear somewhat fussy and fragmented by comparison with those of a century or a century and a half earlier; the single over-arching vision that had characterized the early Gothic buildings had gone. But a building is never less than an expression of the values of the age that gave birth to it. And, in the late Middle Ages, it was very much individual values that were to the fore. The older collectivities were weakening. Opportunities for advancement were more numerous. Mobility, both social and geographical, was on the increase. There was a greater premium now on display. Individuals felt the need to leave their mark on the world; and commissioning fine objects was one way of doing this. If their efforts were sometimes brash and assertive in style, they were rarely entirely lacking in quality or worth. As the Age of Chivalry merged into the Age of the Renaissance, English culture, though lacking the youthful promise of early Gothic, was still as vibrant and creative as it had ever been.

II KNIGHTLY CODES AND PIETY

Juliet and Malcolm Vale

Edward the Black Prince (d. 1376), eldest son of Edward III, might be held in many ways to epitomize the ideal of English chivalry. Distinguished in individual feats of arms at an early age, he went on to achieve equal renown as a commander, notably at the battles of Poitiers (1356) and Nájera (1367); Froissart called him 'the flower of the world's knighthood at that time and the most successful soldier of his age'. Looking at his tomb in Canterbury Cathedral with the effigy of the prince in armour, the chest emblazoned with his coat of arms, badges, mottoes and devices; the helm, crest and surcoat magificently embroidered with his coat of arms placed triumphantly above it we are struck by the full force of what appears to be the worldly display of secular values.

Yet this is only one visual strand. The effigy's own eyes are fixed in death on the image of the Trinity painted on the ceiling, or tester, above him. This painting has deteriorated badly over the centuries, but has been skilfully reconstructed. In it God the Father sits enthroned above the world, with the crucified Christ between his knees and outstretched arms, whilst the Holy Spirit in the form of a dove flies from his mouth. (This distinctive iconography is known as a *Gnadenstuhl* Trinity.) For the Black Prince there can be no doubt that this image transcended the heraldic display on the outside of his tomb. This is emphasized by the epitaph which he instructed in his will should be placed 'on our tomb, in a place where it may be most clearly read and seen', including the lines:

Effigy of the Black Prince in Canterbury Cathedral (c. 1376) showing his helm with leopard crest and the arms of war upon his surcoat.

> On earth I had great riches, which gave me great nobility,
> Lands, houses, great treasures, fine cloths, horses, silver and gold.
> But now I am a poor caitiff, laid deep in the earth.

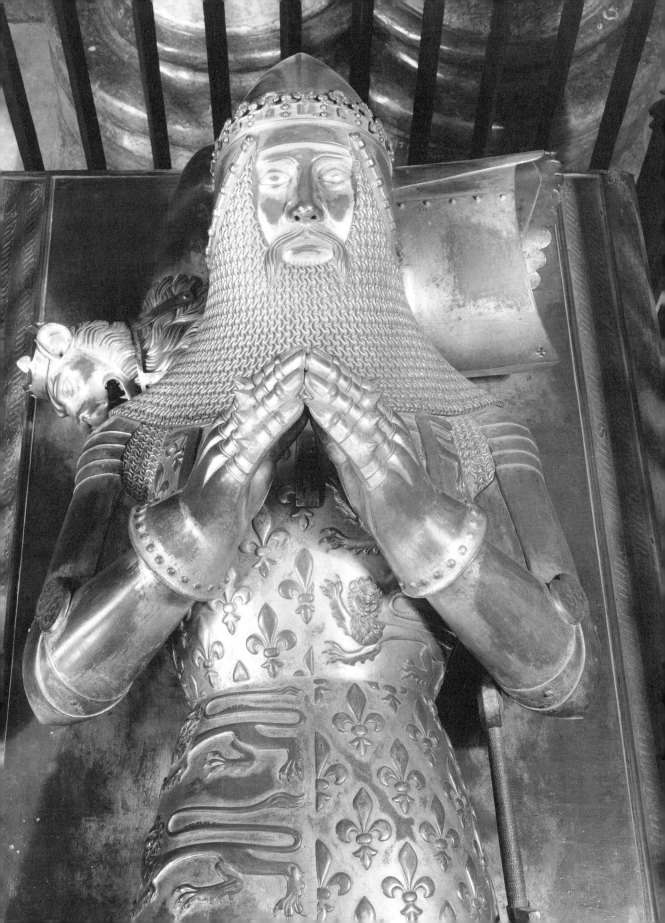

His devotion to the Trinity almost certainly stemmed from his own birth on Trinity Sunday and we know the festival was celebrated magnificently in the prince's household. It is clear that this was a long-standing devotion: the illuminated frontispiece of a manuscript of Chandos Herald's verse biography of the prince shows him kneeling beneath a *Gnadenstuhl* Trinity — a motif also found on a lead badge in the British Museum — and the document granting the English duchy of Aquitaine to the prince in 1364 has an initial decorated with a *Gnadenstuhl* Trinity. His long illness also drew to a close on Trinity Sunday and it was no coincidence that the prince had founded a chantry chapel, where two priests were to say masses for his soul after his death, in the cathedral church of the Holy Trinity at Canterbury.

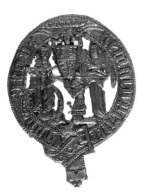

The Black Prince kneels before the Trinity as angels present his shield and crested helm on this lead Garter badge, probably worn in his funeral procession (c. 1376).

The Black Prince's devotion to the Trinity seems to have been well known in his own day, with allusions to it in contemporary proclamations and sermons, but we can do no more than glimpse it occasionally. There is rather more evidence for the devotional practice of his father's friend and relative Henry, Duke of Lancaster (*c.* 1310–61), not least because in 1354 he composed a devotional work, *Le Livre de Seyntz Medecines* (The Book of Holy Cures). This is an allegorical and penitential work in which conventional themes, such as Christ the physician healing the wounds of sin, or the metaphor of the body as a castle, are invigorated by personal experience — in the tournament, battle, siege and everyday life. Lancaster had been involved in war and diplomacy at the highest levels in the early stages of the Hundred Years War and his attachment to the chivalric code is reflected in the authorship of a book (which has not survived) on the laws of war.

Even without *Le Livre de Seyntz Medecines* the number of gifts and endowments made to religious houses and his own foundations testify to Lancaster's piety. Of particular importance to him was the college of secular canons that he established in the Newarke at Leicester. Provision was made for no fewer than a hundred paupers with ten women to look after them, while the collegiate church was served by a dean and a dozen canons and vicars choral, with other clerics.

The ascetic cast of mind that stipulated their sombre black, white and grey garments is also to be found in Lancaster's instructions for his funeral, set out in his will. The coffin was to be accompanied by fifty paupers carrying tapers and he gave strict instructions that there was to be 'nothing vain nor extravagant' and warned specifically against the contemporary practice of armed men bearing his coats of arms riding with them — of which more later.

A similarly penitent spirit may have been responsible for the Norfolk tombs of Sir Roger de Kerdiston and Sir Oliver de Ingham (d. 1337, 1344).

In each case the knight's effigy lies, oddly contorted, upon a bed of pebbles covering the tomb chest. We know that Ingham (who had been seneschal and then lieutenant of the duchy of Aquitaine) petitioned the pope for licence to choose his own confessor and to have a portable altar, for permission to have mass said at such an altar in places which lay under papal interdict and to have mass said before daybreak. Ingham's conscience may have been particularly restless because of his part in the summary execution of one of the murderers of Edward II.

A knightly testator would often leave detailed instructions for the decoration of his tomb, as well as for the funeral ceremony. The Yorkshire Garter knight, Sir Brian Stapleton, stipulated in 1394 that there should be at his funeral 'a man armed with my arms, with my helm on his head . . . well mounted and a man of good appearance'.

Nearly fifty years earlier, John de Warenne, Earl of Surrey, desired in 1347 that no fewer than four horses should precede his hearse, two with horse and rider in his arms of war and two in his arms of peace (worn at the tournament). This was common practice in the fourteenth and fifteenth centuries and one or more of the horses with the arms of war would usually be given to the church where the knight was buried, together with his helm, crest and surcoat, which were displayed above his tomb.

This is why the Black Prince's accoutrements are displayed above his tomb, for his body had been preceded by two destriers (warhorses) and two men 'armed in our arms and our helms'. One was armed with the quartered arms of England and France that the prince had borne in time of war, the other in his 'arms of peace' — three ostrich feathers on a black ground, a device familiar today as 'the Prince of Wales's feathers'. As instructed, his tomb chest was decorated alternately with six shields of peace and six shields of war. The Black Prince also followed common later medieval practice in leaving a set of fine black hangings, in which the ostrich-feather badge was the dominant motif, to various altars in the cathedral: there was clearly nothing incongruous about the introduction of his arms into such a setting. At Gloucester Cathedral, Maurice de Berkeley had filled the great east window with the arms of himself and his peers who had fought at the battle of Crécy (1346) and siege of Calais (1347). The visual intertwining of what we might label 'secular' and 'religious' reflects their fusion in the chivalric mentality.

A knight's coat of arms, his 'arms of war', was essentially unchanging and hereditary. This was his distinguishing mark in times of warfare — on campaign, at siege or on the battlefield itself. The 'arms of peace', which the knight wore at tournaments and jousts where blunted weapons were employed, were quite different because the badge was individual (although relatives might choose to wear similar devices) and a knight might be associated with a number of different badges. We know, for instance, that the Black Prince rode in tournament teams with badges of the Garter and also of a golden eagle on a red ground.

Edward III was associated with a complex series of iconographical themes — pheasants, mermaids, a wreath of honeysuckle, the motto, 'It is as it is', as well as the sunburst and the Garter. The Garter itself demonstrates the fluid context of such devices: the motto, '*Honi soit qui mal y pense* (shame to him who thinks ill of it)', was probably adopted as the king's device for his French campaign in 1346 and his claim to the French Crown, but it could also be used as an occasional tournament badge, as well as providing the

The king enthroned and surrounded by knights and clerks: an allegory of the relationship between Crown, Church and kingdom. From Walter de Milemete's, De nobilitatibus *(c. 1326).*

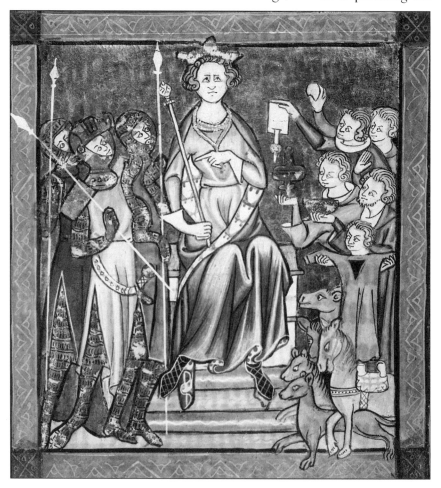

insignia for the Order of the Garter. Context was important in determining whether a badge was ephemeral or whether it achieved more permanent status. Moreover, relatively few individuals would have had the necessary material resources to commission new emblems with the frequency of the king.

The 'arms of peace' were a natural consequence of the use of blunted weapons on occasion at tournaments and jousts from the late thirteenth century onwards. The tournament at this date was, broadly speaking, an armed encounter between two groups of knights over a defined area (a level meadow outside a city or castle was a traditionally popular site), while the joust was a combat between two individual knights. Both provided an opportunity for testing and display.

It would be mistaken to assume from their popularity that these were essentially recreational activities. The joust provided training in one-to-one combat and the handling of horse and weapons, and reflected contemporary technical developments. It became appreciably more hazardous in the second half of the fourteenth century with the adoption of the 'lance-rest', a prong on the right side of the breast plate which supported and steadied the lance. Longer, heavier lances were then employed and the introduction of the tilt barrier between the two combatants in the 1420s was a response to this increased danger.

Throughout the later Middle Ages, the tournament provided the training ground for the mounted knight. This was where he could combine his individual prowess with the group skills required in war, especially following and rallying behind the banners and pennons which were so important in medieval warfare, since their movement in effect dictated the course of a battle. We know that knights of the Black Prince's household — amongst them Sir John Chandos and Sir James Audley — who fought close to him in battle did so in the tournament as well. Contracts between lord and retainer also survive, stipulating service in both war and tournament.

The tournament was also an arena for the conscious practice and display of knightly virtues. The individual knight could demonstrate his own prowess, his loyalty to his comrades and to his lord, his honour and *courtoisie* (courtesy) in observance of the codes relating to such matters as treatment of fallen opponents or the capture of horses. For the lord, it was also an opportunity for the conspicuous *largesse* (generosity) towards his followers that was expected of him. In *Le Livre de Seyntz Medecines*, Henry of Lancaster related how he deliberately cut a fine figure at the tournament in order to impress the ladies present — though he adds significantly that neither tournament nor jousting are intrinsically sinful.

Nevertheless, the tournament could be an extremely dangerous activity: Henry of Lancaster also refers to the frequent blows on the nose sustained by a man who had been to many tournaments. Indeed, when 'jousts of war' were held between the English and the Scots at Roxburgh in 1341, in the course of the Anglo-Scots war, Lancaster and his companions fatally wounded three Scottish knights. Casualties also occurred in much less antagonistic contexts: William, Count of Hainault, Holland and Zeeland (brother-in-law of Edward III), was wounded at a tournament at Eltham in 1342 and John of Beaumont (another Hainaulter, long an active supporter of Edward III) was killed at Northampton the same year. The Eltham tournament formed part of the celebrations to mark the visit of William of Hainault. Tournaments often accompanied ceremonial occasions of this kind: betrothals, marriages, baptisms and churchings, as well as victories, were all celebrated in this way. Royal household accounts often provide detailed evidence for these occasions: there was a striking red and green theme for the baptism of William of Windsor in 1348, with a green bed of state for the baby (in his green-covered cradle) and a red one for the queen, whose chamber was hung with red silk hangings patterned all over with the letter S.

There was a strong mimetic element in many tournaments. At Smithfield in 1343, the inspiration was topical: a pope and twelve cardinals took on all comers at a period when the election of Pope Clement VI had resulted in a marked pro-French shift in papal policy. At the same period, very similar articles were provided as props for the king's *ludi* (probably dramatic games) at Christmas and Epiphany and for tournaments. Crests for some of the founder-members of the Garter (such as the leaves of a plant issuant from a flower pot or the man's head in profile with asses' ears of Neil Loring and Jean de Grailly) would be appropriate in either context.

Many of the themes which inspired chivalric display of this kind stemmed from Arthurian romance. A clear romance inspiration, for instance, lay behind the celebration of Edward I's successful Welsh campaign in 1284. This took the form of a 'round table' at Nefyn, on the Welsh coast not far from Caernarfon. Tournaments were often part of several days' festivities that also involved jousts and dancing; at a round table they had a specifically Arthurian colour. In chivalric culture throughout Europe, Wales was synonymous with the triumph of romance over all that was strange and marvellous. We know from an Italian writer whom he met in Sicily that Edward I enjoyed Arthurian romance and *Escanor*, one of the romances continuing the story of the Arthurian knights, was presented to his consort, Queen Eleanor. Some of the prestige of the Arthurian legend was transferred to English knights: a contemporary French poem describing a

Armed figure of Hugh Despenser, the Younger (d. 1326): stained glass from Tewkesbury Abbey, c. 1340–4.

30

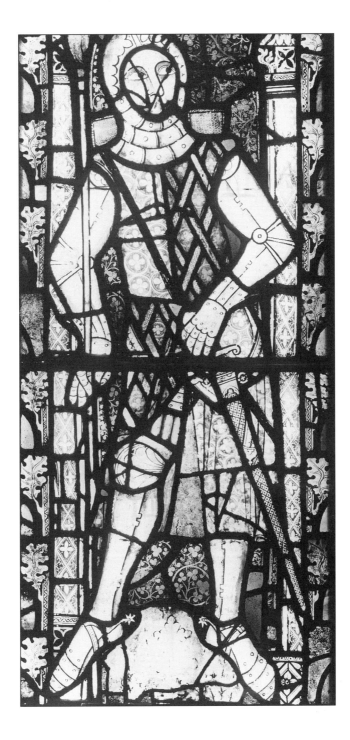

tournament says that the best jousters are to be found in England, juxtaposing the hope that Edward I will attend with the names of Arthurian heroes. Edward was well aware of the advantages of this association: in 1278 the entire court attended the exhumation of the supposed tombs of Arthur and Guinevere at Glastonbury Abbey and their solemn reburial in front of the high altar, while the crown of Arthur was presented to him after the defeat of the Welsh.

Edward I's grandson, Edward III, was to pursue this theme, announcing the foundation in 1344 of a round table for up to 300 knights to be held at Windsor the following Whitsun. The choice of Pentecost, the solemn oath and announcement after mass in the castle chapel all echo Arthurian romance, while the succession of oaths sworn by knights and nobles is reminiscent of the institution of the quest of the Holy Grail at Arthur's court. Although it is not clear how far these plans were carried out, the famous round table in the Great Hall of Winchester Castle now dated *c.* 1260–90 may have been associated with these ceremonies.

Like his grandfather, Edward III was well aware of the political advantage that accrued from such a display, but there can be little doubt that he was personally inspired by the ideals of Arthurian chivalry. At the tournament held at Dunstable in 1342 to celebrate the betrothal of his son Lionel, the king chose to joust as an ordinary knight (*miles simplex*) — a favourite ploy of the most renowned Arthurian knights when they wished to remain incognito. Interestingly, we know from royal household accounts that Edward III chose to appear in the arms of 'Monsieur Lionell' at an earlier Dunstable tournament (1334). This occasion was recorded in a roll of arms where there is no mention of the king and 'Monsieur Lyonel' is recorded just as any other knight present. Edward's choice of Lionel (cousin of Lancelot) may have been influenced by a punning association with the leopards of the English royal arms. The great and enduring popularity of the Arthurian romances had led to the creation of an entirely spurious Arthurian heraldry by this date, with which Edward III and his court were clearly familiar.

Edward III's chivalric foundation, the Order of the Garter and the collegiate chapel of St George at Windsor (1348), also embodied romance ideals. One clause of the Order's statutes stipulates that any candidate must be of noble birth and a *chevalier sans reproche* (of irreproachable honour). Rank affected such matters as fees paid upon an individual's entry to the Order and the number of obituary masses said after his death, but not the relationship between members — a new member was received as an equal, *amy, frere et compaignon* (friend, brother and companion). It was also expressly

Choir of St George's Chapel, Windsor, hung with banners of twentieth-century successors to Edward III's Garter knights.

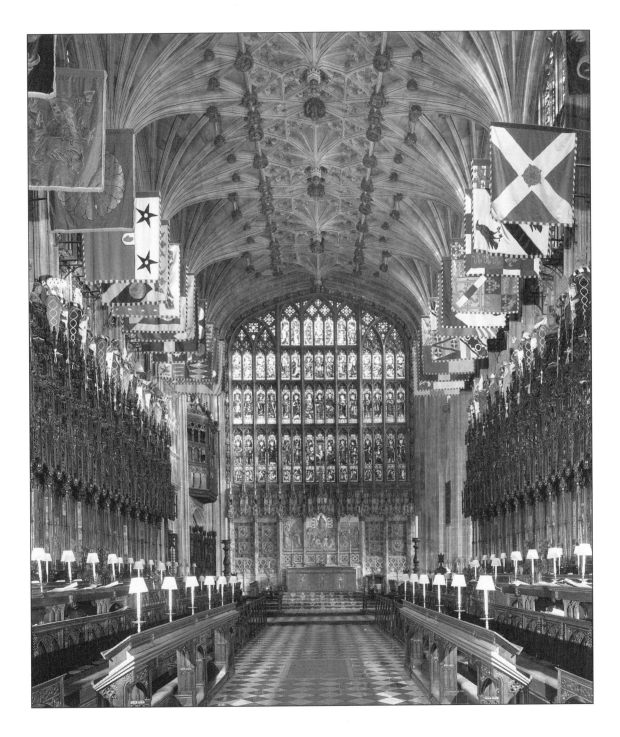

stated that the rank of the member was not to influence seating in the chapel of St George — a knight of the Order occupied the same stall there for the rest of his life, whatever his status or that of the previous holder.

Their annual celebration of the feast of St George included a formal meeting on the eve of the saint's day at which the conduct of both candidates for the Order and existing members was scrutinized in the light of the chivalric code. Feats of arms — and, occasionally, grounds for degradation — were probably recorded in a lost roll of honour or chronicle of the Order of the Garter. For example, in April 1429, Sir John Radcliffe was elected to the Order and replaced the suspended Sir John Fastolf, whose behaviour was not deemed exemplary, after Radcliffe's sponsors had submitted a written account of his merits. This has survived in one of the manuscripts belonging to Elias Ashmole (historian of the Garter in the seventeenth century) and was almost certainly extracted from a larger work containing other such narratives.

However often it was sinned against in practice, the code of chivalry was the foundation and touchstone of these knights' everyday life. Most important of all was the indissoluble link between chivalry and Christian belief: the Garter knight's helm and sword were left above his stall in the chapel of St George at Windsor, not as a manifestation of individual honour and prowess, but primarily *en defense de saincte eglise* (in defence of holy Church), knighthood's primary aim.

This was a conventional and long-established view of its function. The Church's greater tolerance of tournaments in the later Middle Ages, for example, represented a concession to the secular nobility whose protection and patronage it was obliged to seek. The religious dimension of knighthood may have seemed dated or hypocritical to later critics, but there is no reason to doubt the conviction with which it was held by the Garter knights. Suspicion of heresy, for instance, constituted grounds for expulsion from all secular orders of chivalry at this date.

In the annual ceremonies of the Garter, the liturgical and secular were interwoven in a fabric in which both elements were vital and the chapel of St George a focal point. Every year there was a vigil and vespers were followed by the Order's chapter and communal meal; on St George's day itself, solemn mass was followed by *disner* and tournament; the proceedings concluded with vespers and the next day the knights were not to depart without special permission before the requiem mass for the souls of deceased members. The clause in the Garter statutes permitting a knight of the Order — or indeed any other knight with the members' agreement — to take up residence in the college of St George at Windsor, at his own expense, reflects the part the Order was undoubtedly expected to play in the members' personal devotions. This was underlined by the fact that they were absolved from wearing the Garter collar on such occasions as a long journey, or during war or sickness, but were expected instead to wear a cord or lace with a pendant figure of St George. It was undoubtedly anticipated that the soldier-saint would be a natural object of the knight's devotion, especially at such times as these.

The Order of the Garter flourished well beyond the end of the Middle Ages. Henry VIII revised its statutes, adopting some practices of the Burgundian Order of the Golden Fleece (1430), and ensured its survival as a national order of chivalry. In 'Gothic' England (1300–1500) the great magnates might distribute livery collars and badges to their retainers, but there were no baronial orders of chivalry on the French or German pattern. The Garter remained essentially the sovereign's order and the Crown's monopoly over England's 'national' chivalry was a striking feature of English political and social development. Despite dynastic upheaval and religious turmoil, lines of continuity between Edward III, the Black Prince and the Tudors can be traced in this aspect of the Crown's relationship with its noble and knightly subjects. In 1538, two years after the first Act for the Dissolution of the Monasteries, the Marquis of Exeter had in his possession two pendants of St George — one on his Garter collar, the other on a lace — a roll and two books of the Garter statutes, a roll of arms of the Garter knights and a plate decorated with 'a scutcheon of St George'. Chivalry and its attendant devotional cults remained a way of life for the English nobility and gentry well into the so-called New Era of the early modern state.

III 'FORGET-ME-NOTS'

Patronage in Gothic England

Nigel Saul

O F THE MANY TREASURES in the National Gallery few have preserved their secrets as successfully as the Wilton Diptych. Its date, its provenance, its meaning have all aroused controversy. Only its beauty is uncontested. The essence of the problem lies in the Christian symbolism of the two wings of the altarpiece. Artistically they form a single composition. Richard II, shown kneeling in the left-hand panel, reaches out to receive the banner of St George being handed to him by the Christ Child depicted in the panel opposite. The gaze of the king, and of the three saints sponsoring him, is directed towards the Child, and that of the latter towards the banner which he is preparing to take from an attending angel. All are enveloped in a mood of mystical dreaminess accentuated by the fact that no two pairs of eyes actually meet each other.

The youthful appearance of the king and the representation of exactly eleven angels in attendance on the Mother and Child have given rise to the suggestion that the subject of the diptych is Richard's coronation, which took place in 1377 when he was eleven years of age. But the employment of the white hart, a device which Richard did not adopt until 1390, suggests otherwise. Altogether more plausible is John Palmer's hypothesis that it portrays Richard vowing to lead a crusade. The badges worn by Richard and the angels facing him — his own white hart and the French king's broom-cod — date it to the period of Anglo-French co-operation in the mid-1390s when a joint crusading force was under consideration: in which case the emblems of the Passion displayed by the Christ Child on his halo must refer to his lost patrimony which Richard, by accepting the banner of Redemption, is indicating his readiness to win back. The commissioning of the diptych can thus be seen as a sign of the English king's resolve to fulfil the commitment into which he and the French king had jointly entered.

The choir of Tewkesbury Abbey, part of an ambitious programme of rebuilding probably paid for by Hugh Despenser, Edward II's favourite.

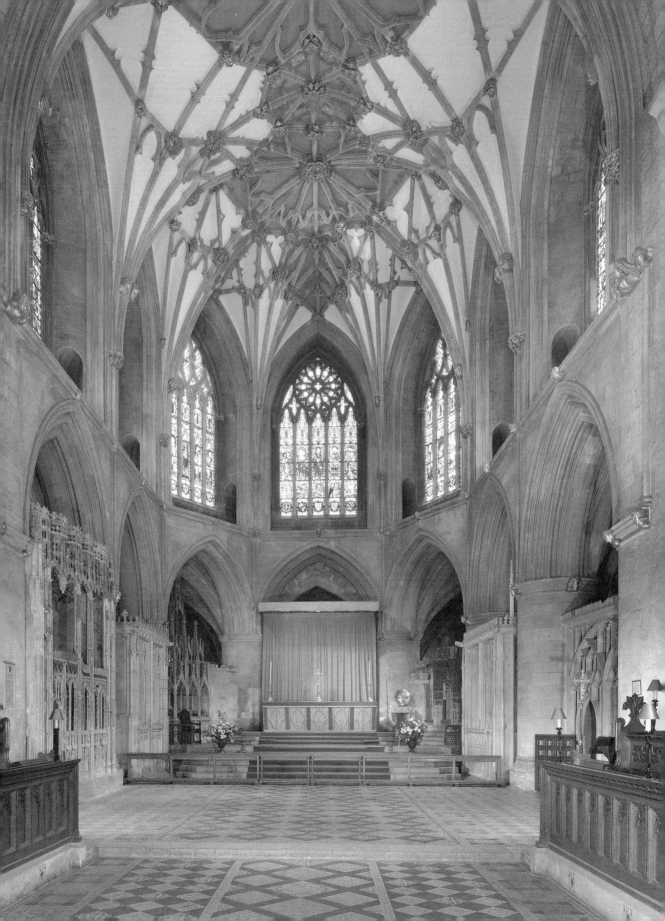

If the symbolism of the diptych allows us to place it in a fairly precise historical context, the inability to identify any of the painters who worked on it frustrates any attempt to place it in an artistic one. The anonymity to which the diptych painters and others like them have been condemned is the unfortunate result, not only of the loss of contemporary documents, but also of the relatively low esteem in which their craft was held. Art in the Middle Ages was principally Christian art. Its purpose was not the exaltation of the artist but the glorification of God. It was conceived, not as an expression of the artist's own personality, but as a vision of the world to come. What value it had was therefore derived less from the skill or sensitivity with which it was executed than from the quality of the insight that it afforded into the kingdom of Heaven. Given this view of the purpose of art, there was little possibility of seeing the artist as an instrument of man's own creativity. It was from God that he derived his inspiration; and it was to God, accordingly, that he dedicated his work. Outside the context provided by the Christian religion, artistic activity was all but inconceivable.

The view that human works could only be appreciated in so far as they revealed some aspect of the world to come was, of course, Platonic in origin. In art, as in philosophy, it led men to place greater value on authority than on originality. Buildings or artefacts excited admiration less for any inherent qualities they had than for their similarity to some widely admired exemplar and for their capacity to inspire devotion in the faithful. Thus the new abbey of St Denis, near Paris, drew from its founder, Abbot Suger, feelings of devotion bordering on ecstasy:

> [It] has overwhelmed me [he said], and the charm of the multi-coloured gems [of the reliquaries] has led me to reflect on the diversity of the sacred virtues ... it seems to me that I can see myself residing in some strange region of the universe which had no previous existence either in the clay of this earth or in the purity of the heavens, and that by the grace of God I can be transported mystically from life on this earth to the higher realm.

Suger, though a pioneer in matters of style, was fairly conventional in matters of theology. His belief that art was a medium for the greater glorification of God was one that was shared by most patrons. It found an echo in the feelings of awe which the monks of Canterbury are recorded as having experienced when they beheld the new vault raised over their choir in the 1170s. 'It seemed to all of us who saw it,' wrote Gervase of Canterbury, 'that it was incomparable and most praiseworthy.'

Honest toil; the figure of an anonymous stonemason in a 1313 stained glass window from St Mary Magdalen's, Helmdon, Northamptonshire – one of the few glimpses in art of the techniques and craftsmen who created it.

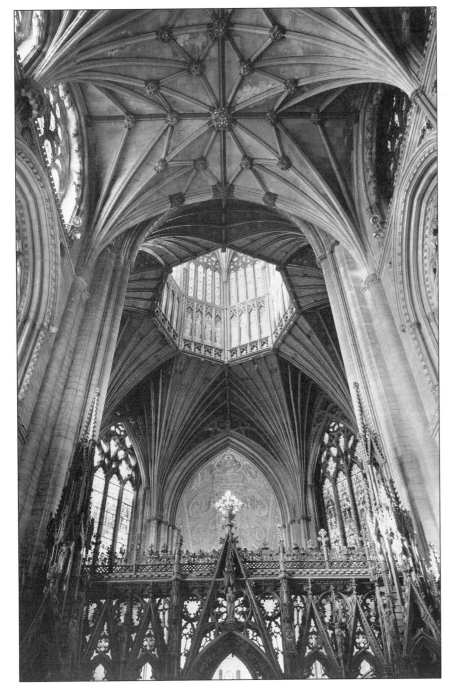

The octagon ceiling at Ely, the work of Alan of Walsingham, the fourteenth-century sacristan of the cathedral.

This was a less intellectualized sort of admiration than that which Suger had experienced. It was the response of a body of men accustomed to observing, rather than participating in, the process of artistic invention. For the most part, the roles of patron and artist were sharply differentiated: the patron was concerned with commissioning works, and the artist with executing them. But just occasionally the two could come together in the person of one uniquely talented polymath. Such a man was probably Alan of Walsingham, the fourteenth-century sacrist of Ely, whom the cathedral chronicler credits with conceiving the great octagonal space in the centre of the church. Walsingham was noted as well for his skill in goldsmith's work. He was, in the best sense of the word, an 'amateur', not a 'professional', and would have relied on the masons and carpenters to draw up the detailed plans and to see them through to completion. But, even so, there is little reason to doubt his responsibility for the initial conception. Roles that were usually separate merged here into a collaborative relationship exceptionally fruitful in its artistic results.

A different aspect of the relationship between patron and artist is illustrated by the history of the rebuilding programme that took place at Tewkesbury Abbey in the early fourteenth century. The choir of this church, which has for long suffered by comparison with the slightly later (and better known) edifice not far away at Gloucester, is one of the most exuberant works of the Decorated style in England. The glorious lierne vault, for which it is chiefly famous, is only the most spectacular feature of an ambitious programme which also included the remodelling of the ambulatory and the creation of a series of enormous traceried windows in the clerestory.

Stylistically, the work has many affinities with that of a group of masons who operated in the south-east of England. Such tell-tale details as the miniature crenellations that are sometimes employed on the turrets, the decorative quatrefoils that appear on some of the tombs and the mouldings used on some of the canopy arches link Tewkesbury with monuments like St Stephen's Chapel in the palace of Westminster and the great royal tombs in the abbey there. These were all works on which members of the de Canterbury family were engaged, and if they (or members of their workshop) were also employed at Tewkesbury, at the very least in a consultative capacity, it could only have been through the patronage extended by the lord of the manor — the king's chamberlain, Hugh Despenser the younger. Despenser had acquired the manor of Tewkesbury in 1317 by his marriage to Eleanor, one of the sisters and co-heiresses of Gilbert de Clare, Earl of Gloucester. Anxious to establish himself as the legitimate successor of his wife's illustrious forebears, he set about remodelling and embellishing the great abbey church in which they had been buried. To this end, he employed the best artistic and architectural talent that money (and his connections at court) could buy. Masons and craftsmen from Westminster, Kent, perhaps even Sussex, were contracted to come to Tewkesbury to create an image of Paradise that would do credit to their great patron.

For a while the abbey enjoyed the distinction of being the most prestigious building in England, but within a few years that distinction had passed to Gloucester, ten miles to the south. The remodelling of the choir there, in a version of the court style that made Tewkesbury's look outmoded, set new standards of taste and artistic excellence. The Decorated style had given way to the Perpendicular, the sinewy to the rigidly rectilinear. Sculpture no less than architecture was affected by this aesthetic revolution and, in the canopy raised over the tomb of the murdered Edward II at Gloucester, the new style established a model that was to provide fertile inspiration for over half a century. Within a few years, a similar forest of pinnacles was to be raised at Tewkesbury over the effigy of Sir Hugh Despenser III (d. 1349), the nephew of Edward II's favourite. He or his widow — whichever of the two commissioned the monument — must surely have been familiar with the Gloucester exemplar and requested a similar design for their own commission. By then the wheel had turned full circle: the lords of Tewkesbury, having set a fashion in the 1320s, found themselves following it in the 1340s.

The choirs of Gloucester and Tewkesbury can both be termed, however loosely, products of the 'court school' in the sense that they were executed by, or embodied the designs of, masons whose chief employment was on royal projects — notably, at this time, St Stephen's Chapel, Westminster. But, of the two, only Gloucester was the beneficiary of direct royal favour. Tewkesbury stood at one remove, being the beneficiary of private patronage. Yet the work carried out at Tewkesbury yielded little if anything in size and splendour to that carried out at the sister abbey. What the king could do it is clear that his magnates could do equally as well. The Beauchamp Chapel at Warwick, the FitzAlan Chapel at Arundel, the parish churches built by the de la Poles at Wingfield and Ewelme, the numerous castles — better to call them stately homes — built by the Percys at Warkworth and Alnwick and by the Nevilles at Raby add up to a programme of construction that puts the nobility on a par with the Crown as patrons of building and art.

The nobility, moreover, were generally able to see their buildings through to fairly speedy conclusion. The king was not. The various prestige projects he initiated (projects which were certainly important in the dissemination of

Here shewes howe king henry the vj. made Erle Richard his
lieutenaunt of ffraunce and Normandy

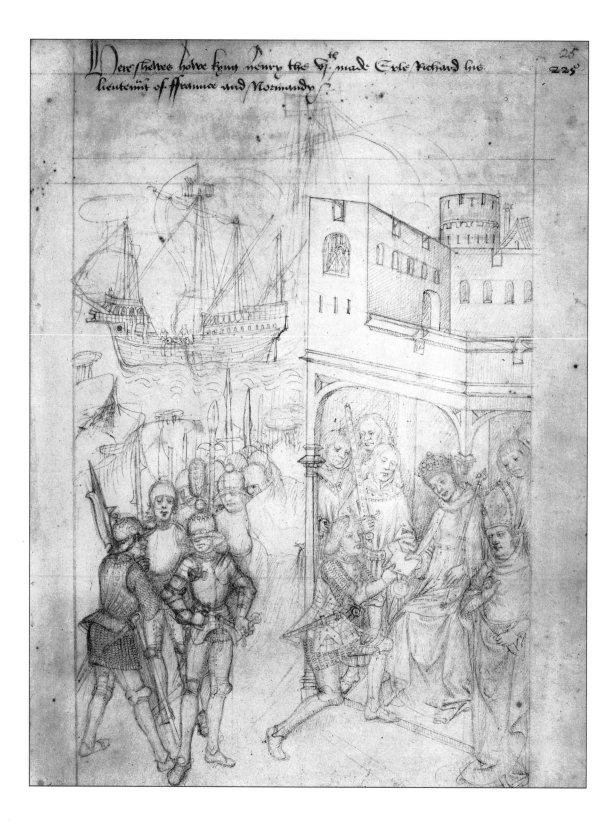

style) were all subject to the vicissitudes of political misfortune. The rebuilding of Westminster Abbey, for example, begun by Henry III in 1245, took a century and three-quarters to complete: interrupted by the Barons' Wars of the 1260s, it was taken up again in the 1360s, but finished only in the fifteenth century by Henry V. The construction of King's College Chapel, Cambridge, had a similarly chequered history. This, the pet project of Henry VI, was begun in the 1440s, but fell victim to the Wars of the Roses, was resumed by Edward IV, and then finally completed, nearly a century after its foundation, by Henry VIII in the 1530s.

Royal patronage could turn out, therefore, to be something of a mixed blessing. Much depended on the initiative of individual monarchs, and not all were as committed as Henry III or Henry VI. Moreover, even if the commitment was there, the money might not be. By the thirteenth century, income from the royal demesne had been severely eroded by inflation, and parliamentary taxation proved inadequate as a substitute because it could be used only for the common weal and not for the king's personal gratification. By comparison with the King of France, the King of England cut a relatively modest figure as a patron. In the mid-fourteenth century, in the person of Edward III, he performed somewhat better, because the fortunes of war placed in his hands two royal captives, the ransoms for whom provided him with a major source of private income. But this advantage did not last, and, by the mid-fifteenth century, the disparity in resources between the two Crowns had become increasingly pronounced. In late medieval England, building programmes on the scale of those initiated by the French kings — such as that undertaken by St Louis at St Denis and the Ste Chapelle — could be contemplated only exceptionally; and on the occasions when they *were* undertaken, as in the reign of Edward III, they did not necessarily allow much scope for work of a strictly artistic nature.

In any society, then, artistic patronage is the product of the interplay of personal fancy and economic circumstance. In France, the two came together most fruitfully in the setting of the court. There, in the late fourteenth century, the learning of Charles V gave encouragement to the production of books, and the aesthetic sensibilities of his brother John, Duke of Berry, to the illumination of manuscripts. In England, by contrast, no one setting predominated. Patronage, like the wealth which made it possible, was dispersed. It manifested itself less in the splendour of a few outstanding works than in the rich variety of the many. Few works of the very highest quality were commissioned — at least, few that can bear comparison with the finest commissioned on the continent. But the lack of distinction, not to say the mediocrity, of much of the rest is in itself revealing of changes in the

An everyday tale of chivalric folk; Richard Beauchamp is made lieutenant of Normandy — a late fifteenth-century illustration from the Warwick Roll, drawn up by John Rous.

pattern of patronage that led to a slow but steady deterioration in standards. No area of activity illustrates this more clearly than the history of manuscript illumination.

The spread of literacy among the upper and middle classes (if they may be so called) generated a large and growing demand for books. Reading matter of all kinds was consumed. Some of it was devotional in character, but much of it was not. Romances, chronicles, histories and ballads were as popular as psalters and books of hours, and among the nobility and gentry, who were appreciating the newly found privacy of the solar or withdrawing room, reading matter enjoyed a vogue approaching that of the present-day novel. Literature of this sort rarely circulated in de luxe manuscripts of the kind we associate with the twelfth century. More commonly, they took the form of quires or booklets produced in urban ateliers which the owner could put together (as Sir John Paston did his) in composite volumes.

Few of these productions have any claim to be esteemed for their artistic excellence. Quite the contrary, the great majority bear ample witness to the coarsening of quality that accompanied the attempt to satisfy what was rapidly becoming a form of mass market. The more lavish treatment was reserved for devotional works, the grandest of which, like the St Omer Psalter (c. 1300–40), can bear comparison with any manuscript of the twelfth or thirteenth century. For reasons that remain obscure, secular texts were rarely given this degree of attention. Late medieval England can offer few if any counterparts to the lavishly illustrated romances produced in Flanders at the time. Perhaps the heavy day-to-day use to which such texts were likely to be subjected made such expensive decoration inadvisable. Certainly, the only secular works that did receive any embellishment (and then not much) were ones of a genealogical nature that were going to be cherished and passed down from generation to generation. A good example of the genre is the Warwick Roll, drawn up and probably illustrated between 1483 and 1485 by one John Rous to celebrate the deeds of the earls of Warwick. It is attractively executed in the 'tinted outline style'; and, in its concern with matters of genealogy and heraldry, it affords a valuable insight into the priorities of the aristocracy. However, judged as a work of art, it falls short of the highest standards of excellence: the drawing is rough, and the figures are a little naïve. It can be read as a paradigm of the general deterioration in artistic standards which took place in fifteenth-century England — a deterioration not unconnected with the growth of the market. In a phrase, more meant worse.

Roughly similar observations may be made of another area in which the interests of patron and artist overlapped — that of the manufacture and supply of church monuments. The practice of seeking commemoration was one that spread rapidly in the late Middle Ages. It sprang principally from a desire to ease the trials of purgatory. The presence of an effigy in a church served to remind people of the deceased's need for their prayers in assisting the passage of his soul from purgatory to Heaven. At a time when few could read, the effigy was a substitute for an inscription. Later, when literacy increased, it was the all but inevitable accompaniment to one. Usually, it depicted the commemorated in the manner of dress appropriate for one of his rank — armour if he was a knight, mass vestments or a cope if he was a priest, civilian attire if he was a burgess. Among the earliest, that is to say twelfth-century, effigies it is those of priests, chiefly bishops and abbots, which predominate. Among their thirteenth- and fourteenth-century successors, it is probably those of knights and their ladies. Clearly, a practice which had begun among the clerical élite spread quickly to its secular counterpart; and by the later thirteenth century, it had become the common, if not habitual, practice of the aristocracy and richer knights to seek commemoration in this way.

The materials used for these early effigies were chiefly Purbeck marble and freestone. Neither was cheap — certainly not cheap to have transported a long way; and the latter in particular suffered from the additional disadvantage that it lacked durability. Experiments were therefore made in the use of a variety of other mediums, including mosaics, enamels, incised slabs, and bronze and alabaster inlays. But, of these, the one that proved most satisfactory by far was the flat sheet of latten that we know today as the 'brass'. It carried with it a number of advantages. It was convenient — being flat it did not use up much space in the church. It was durable — it did not flake or erode. But above all it was flexible — it could be as large or as small as the client wanted. The very largest brasses were large by any standard, some being twelve to fifteen feet in length; and the smallest likewise were very small — sometimes consisting of no more than an inscription measuring nine inches by three.

Today, of course, it is the larger compositions which attract our attention. The best of them — like that to Abbot Thomas de la Mare in St Alban's Abbey (engraved c. 1360) — rank as some of the finest works of art ever produced in the Middle Ages. But, in the context of the total output of the workshops, they are unrepresentative. The majority commemorated the not-so-great rather than the great. Coming as they did in every shape and size, they could be made to fit every shape and size of pocket. They opened the possibility of commemoration to classes of people who would otherwise have found it beyond their means — to men, that is, like John the Smith of

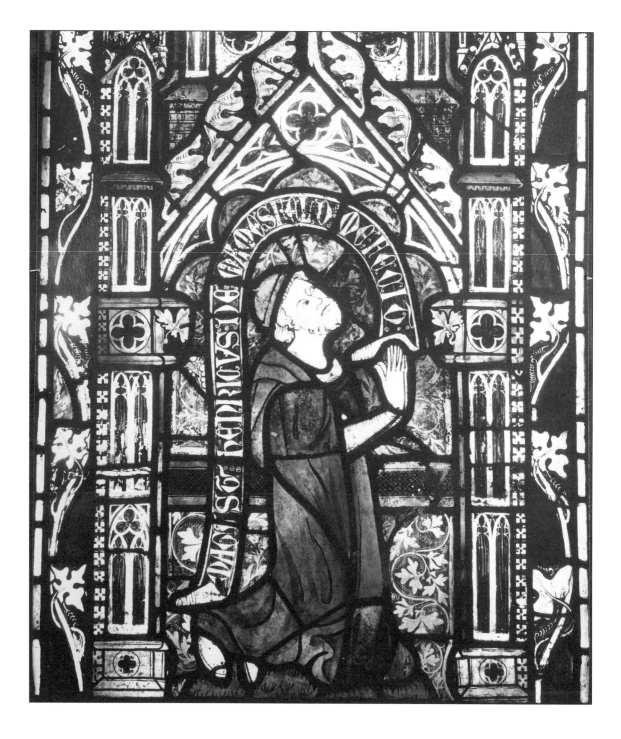

Brightwell Baldwin in Oxfordshire, whose inscription of *c.* 1370 has the honour to be the earliest to survive in the vernacular.

The comparative cheapness of brasses generated a demand which led to the growth of techniques of mass production not unlike those we have observed in the stationery trade. In the fifteenth century, large workshops, most of them situated in London, were turning out hundreds of stock products every year — such variations as there were between them being chiefly those of size rather than of quality. The expansion of the market, which was part cause and part consequence of the overall lowering of costs, made a craft of what had once been craftsmanship, and artisanship of what had once been art. From the strictly artistic point of view, this line of development was doubtless unfortunate; but, from the historical point of view, it is exceedingly instructive. Patronage of culture, never wholly the monopoly of the élite, was becoming ever more widely diffused in society. The general increase in national wealth in the Middle Ages contributed to this, but so too, and probably to a greater degree, did the redistribution of that wealth in the century and a half after the Black Death. The plague of 1348 exacted a heavy toll in lives; but it also raised living standards for those who survived. The scarcity of labour led to a sharp rise in wages, transferring purchasing power to those who had previously lacked it and who were able to move up the social ladder and the expenditure of a modest sum on a few books, an alabaster or a brass was one way of showing that they had 'arrived'.

Patronage in the late Middle Ages, therefore, became the property of the many, but it did not in the process become anonymous or impersonal. On the contrary, the patron pushed himself ever more prominently to the fore. In the case of powerful men like Hugh Despenser the younger at Tewkesbury this is hardly surprising. In the case of lesser men perhaps it is. The evidence is everywhere for us to see — whether in the clerestory of Long Melford Church in Suffolk, where the names of the benefactors are carved in the stonework, or in the stained glass windows of Merton College Chapel, Oxford, where the kneeling figure of Master Henry de Mamesfield appears with monotonous regularity in each of the dozen windows that he paid for. The role of the patron became more explicit, more assertive. If this was mainly a consequence of his ever-present sense of insecurity — of his need to request, as on a brass, prayers for the safety of his soul — it was also a concession to his sense of vanity. Patrons, unlike the artists whom they employed, did not allow their names to become forgotten.

'And now a word from our sponsor . . .'; the kneeling figure of Henry de Mamesfield repeated throughout the stained glass of Merton College Chapel in Oxford, which he commissioned in the late Middle Ages, illustrates the increased demands of patrons to be kept in the picture.

IV ARTISTS AND CRAFTSMEN
Nigel Ramsay

I F A WELL-TO-DO DOWAGER DIED in late fourteenth-century England, how might her son or executor set about commemorating her? As the estates were no longer burdened with her right of dower (by common law one-third of her husband's estate), he could well afford to spend £10 or £20 or more. He could set up a chantry with a priest to pray for her soul and his father's; or he could concentrate his resources on some tangible memorial — perhaps a free-standing carved tomb in the chancel of the local parish church, or a memorial brass, which would be cheaper and might allow funds to stretch to a stained glass window as well. If he decided on the latter combination, how would he actually choose what designs to follow and how would the services or products of competent craftsmen be obtained?

It would have been a straightforward matter to order a memorial brass: the leading English workshop, with almost a monopoly in the market, was based in the churchyard of St Paul's Cathedral, and, the next time business took some local lawyer or merchant to London, he could be commissioned to visit the marbler, who ran the business, give him the wording, or at least the gist of the wording, of an appropriate inscription, and select a suitable design for the figurative part. The marbler would have had several figure designs, of different sizes and cost, and it would have been easiest to select one of these, although an alternative would have been to request a memorial like a particular one that had been erected in some nearby church.

The stained glass window would have been more problematic. There were capable glaziers in several cities and towns, and it might have been simpler to look somewhere other than London. A workshop's master might be known by some commission that he had recently carried out locally, one for a friend or relative, or because he came from the patron's locality: there were various possible avenues to be explored. The design, or at least the subject matter, of the glass needed careful consideration. The deceased's patron saints might be represented, but so might she herself, together with

Alabaster effigies of Sir Ralph Greene (d. 1417) and his wife Katharine at Lowick, Northamptonshire. Made, for £40, by Thomas Prentys and Robert Sutton, carvers, of Chellaston, Derbyshire, 1419–20.

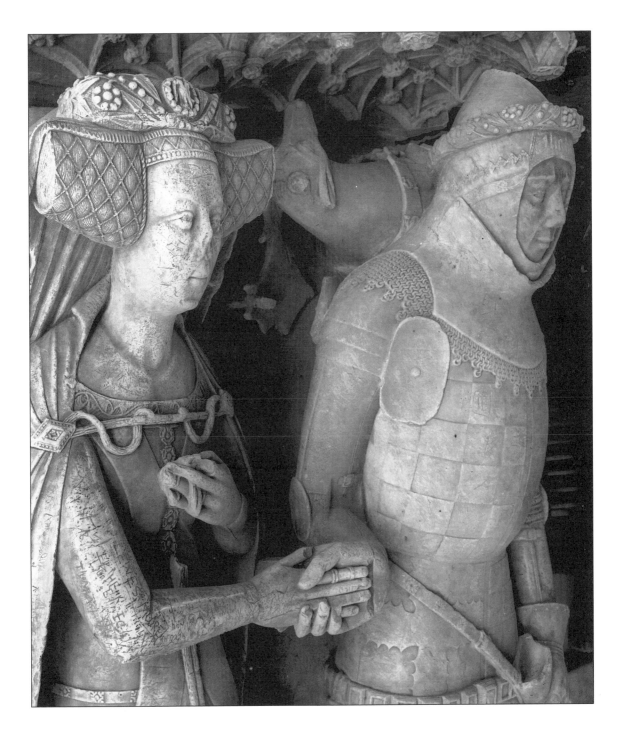

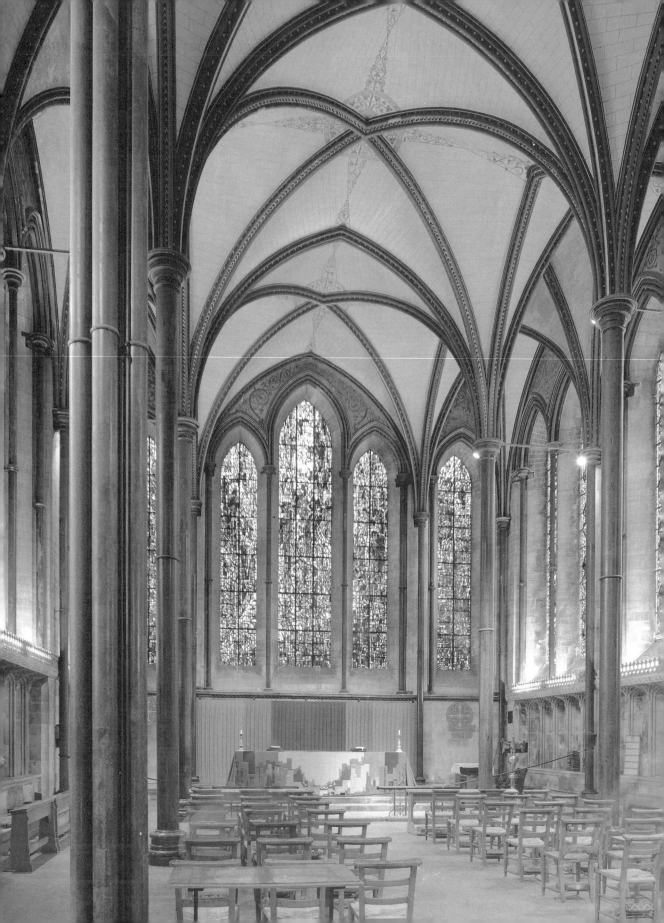

her coat of arms (in conjunction with that of her husband). A visit by the glazier would have been needed, to measure the windows and agree on a suitable design; it might have been convenient to give the commission to the master currently working at the nearest cathedral.

In all this, the last thought to have entered the patron's head would have been whether he was buying a work of artistic originality. He might not have wanted a replica of someone else's memorial brass or stained glass window, but neither of these commissions would have been so common-place that it was likely to be matched already in the parish church. In any case, it was not the habit of medieval craftsmen to produce identical copies, although thanks to the use of stencils brasses were sometimes very similar. The craftsman would work in a particular style, which would reflect both what he had been taught and what he had seen subsequently; his skill lay, however, in his mastery of the techniques that were called for in the production of what he made. This was equally true of the craftsmen whom today we would call artists practising 'fine arts': no distinction was drawn in the Middle Ages between those who drew in books or on wooden panels and those who painted on walls, or who engraved designs on metal, or on a clay or wax mould. Artists and craftsmen were two of a kind. The difference which sometimes emerged, especially towards the close of the Middle Ages, was that between the craftsman and the patron or the patron's representative who so involved himself in the design of a commission as to pose today's art historians with the problem of whether he was the designer or even the creator of what resulted from his involvement. Elias of Dereham, in the early thirteenth century, was just such a patron or amateur: he was one of the two 'incomparable masters . . . by whose counsel and invention everything necessary was done to the making' of St Thomas Becket's shrine at Canterbury Cathedral in 1220, while a few years later he was described as 'director of the new fabric' of Salisbury Cathedral.

In the late nineteenth and early twentieth centuries, much ink was spilt in arguments about how far medieval art was the creation of the Church, or, more particularly, of monks. Elias of Dereham was a secular canon and a 'civil servant' — he was in charge of the king's works at Winchester Castle and Clarendon Palace, Wiltshire, around 1235 — and so was not fair ammunition in this battle. Instead, historians focused their attention on his contemporaries, Matthew Paris and Walter of Colchester (the other master named as helping to make Becket's shrine), who were both monks of St Alban's Abbey. Research has shown that it was rare for monks to be active as craftsmen, save in the arts of the book — and even there to a steadily diminishing degree after the later twelfth or early thirteenth century.

Salisbury Cathedral: the Lady Chapel, built c. 1220–5. Probably designed by Nicholas of Ely; built under the general superintendence of Elias of Dereham.

On the other hand, cathedrals and abbeys were immensely important in the furtherance of all sorts of arts or crafts, especially in the first century or two after the Norman Conquest when so many of the greater churches were being built. The Church was the all-important patron throughout the country, and it must have been because of ecclesiastical patronage that we can read of, say, Durham work, as a particular type of goldsmith's work. Canterbury, too, was a centre for goldsmiths, not least because it had a mint; only one twelfth-century monk of the Cathedral Priory is known to have been a goldsmith, however, and it is possible that he was called 'the goldsmith' simply because he came of a family of goldsmiths. He might better be taken as illustrating the community of interests to which both monks and craftsmen might simultaneously belong — a world in which the service of God was given or enhanced by both sorts of men.

Craftsmanship in the service of God is the leitmotiv of the most helpful surviving medieval craftsman's manual, *Of Divers Arts (De Diversis Artibus)*, written by a German monk called Theophilus in the early twelfth century. It is not easy to reconstruct the working methods of medieval craftsmen, even if their crucibles, kilns or finished works survive and can be subjected to scientific analysis. Craftsmen learnt their skills by serving an apprenticeship, and even if they were literate they did not need a written manual to remind them how to set about their work. Quite a large number of medieval recipes and 'secrets' do survive, together with a few accounts of technical procedures, but these are almost all comprehensible only to people who already know something of the subject. Theophilus's book stands out as having been written for the uninitiated and as setting out a great many of the stages of manufacture of each artefact, being especially detailed in its treatment of metalwork. What he says about the use of colours in book illustration may have been taken from earlier German works (or an old oral tradition), but his account of a wide range of metalworking techniques gives the impression that here he was writing from personal experience, starting with the making of a workshop: 'Build a high spacious building whose length extends to the east. In the south wall put as many windows as you wish and are able to, provided that there is a space of five feet between any two windows . . .' He continues with a description of the table, forge and bellows and the gilding of brass, repoussé work (embossed work) and its chasing, the casting of bells and how to tune them, and the inlaying of iron with gold and silver: 'If you wish to have letters on knives or other things made of iron, engrave them first with an engraving tool, and then, from a thick silver wire that you have made, shape the letters with fine tweezers, lay them in the grooves and embed them by striking them on top with a hammer . . .'

Only one medieval English library is known to have had a copy of Theophilus's work, which survives in a few continental manuscripts; but the techniques that he described were commonly used throughout Europe. The sort of book that does survive in England is the classical treatise of Vitruvius, *On Architecture (De Architectura)*: there are still copies in existence that once belonged, for example, to both the Cathedral Priory and St Augustine's Abbey at Canterbury. It was probably a copy of this work that was bequeathed by a mid-fifteenth-century town clerk of London to his relative, John Carpenter, later Bishop of Worcester. Vitruvius's work would have given a theoretical background for a monk at Canterbury concerned with superintending the fabric of the cathedral. A more practical book, of which five English cathedrals or abbeys are known to have had a copy, was an iconographic treatise, *Pictor in Carmine*, providing collections of theological types and antitypes (complementary scenes from the Old and New Testaments, the former being presented as prefigurations of the latter) — invaluable for the designer of a set of stained glass windows, illustrated manuscripts or wall paintings, or for a patron commissioning them.

The last page of the Table of Subjects and the beginning of the text of Pictor in Carmine. *Copied in the thirteenth century.*

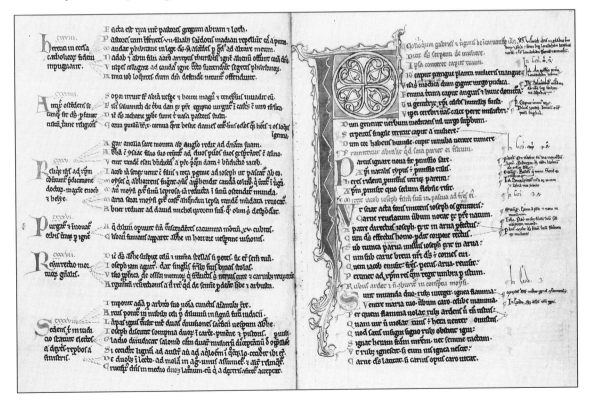

In medieval England only those who worked on the land can have been more numerous than craftsmen. Every village had its craftsmen — a carpenter, or a more specialized woodworker, such as a wheelwright, a blacksmith or a stonemason — and the working populations of towns were largely made up of craftsmen. Shops were kept by purveyors of some sort of foodstuff or by craftsmen who had very likely themselves made a large proportion of what they sold. Regional or, more particularly, local specializations were commonplace, however, being determined partly by the availability of raw materials and partly by the location of consumers. Embroidery flourished in London because the richest patrons found it convenient to place their commissions there and because the silkwomen depended on silk thread imported through London; but most specializations were in other parts of England. In the later twelfth and thirteenth centuries, books were principally written and illustrated at Oxford and Cambridge; in the fourteenth and fifteenth centuries, alabaster pits were extensively worked in Derbyshire and Staffordshire and religious imagery of alabaster was carved in the vicinity of the pits or in the nearby towns, such as Burton-upon-Trent or, later, Nottingham. England was almost the sole European producer of alabaster and of tin (needed for the manufacture of fine pewter and of some copper alloys, notably for bells), and these materials were worked on a large scale, requiring the good communications afforded by fair-sized towns for their full development.

Tradition must have played a part, too: as a place became known for goods of a particular type, other craftsmen might be drawn there by the knowledge that consumers would also be attracted to it. A set of verses of the mid- or late thirteenth century lists English towns with their characteristic products or attributes, and although some of these are humorously intended, like the whores of Charing, by London, others did reflect local specialities — needles at Wilton in Wiltshire, marble, i.e. Purbeck marble, at Corfe in Dorset, and cutlery at Thaxted in Essex.

Beginning in the twelfth century, craftsmen of particular skills in various larger towns began to form groupings or associations. These groupings, generally called gilds (from the Old English *geld*, meaning payment or contribution), owed their existence to the need for the members to be represented in dealings with the Crown or with the other inhabitants of the town. A few gilds, known as 'gilds merchant', actually comprised all the leading merchants and craftsmen of a town and ran the town's general affairs. Most, however, were limited to the practitioners of a particular craft and, inevitably, it was the craftsmen such as fullers and weavers, whose products were the least distinguishable in any personal way, who first came together: their gilds are known to have existed in the twelfth century in such towns as Huntingdon, Lincoln, London, Oxford, Winchester and York, being named in governmental tax records, but part of their *raison d'être* must have been the need to maintain certain standards of production. A consumer could easily weigh up the merits of his local cobbler, but the weavers' cloth might travel far before it found a purchaser. For similar reasons, the goldsmiths of London also formed themselves into a gild, and were fined £30 in 1179–80 for having done so without permission from the Crown; the large size of the fine is slightly surprising, however, because the Crown stood to benefit from the silver coinage being of a consistently high level of purity and depended on goldsmiths for the running of the mint.

Craftsmen who produced works of art had less cause to form gilds. They tended to rely on their personal reputation, and were also more likely to travel around the country. They owed much to their patrons for their popularity and prospects of employment, and often found it more practical to join the household of a nobleman or a bishop if that offered the best prospects. In this case, they remained highly mobile, for such a patron usually owned properties in several places, and might also 'loan' them to other patrons on a temporary basis. For instance, in 1520 Sir Nicholas Vaux wrote to Cardinal Wolsey seeking his help over the buildings to be erected on the occasion of the Field of Cloth of Gold, and requested 'that yt would please your Grace to send hither maister Maynn, who dweleth with the Bisshope of Excestre, and Maistre Barkleye, the Black monke and poete, to devise histoires and convenient raisons to florrisshe the buildings and Banket [i.e., Banqueting] House withal'. Alexander Barclay's task was to produce inscriptions and mottoes, while Maynn, probably to be identified as the Italian Giovanni da Maiano (who subsequently worked for Wolsey on Hampton Court Palace), was to provide the overall scheme, no doubt of representational decoration.

Within the building trade, it was more common for a master mason or master carpenter to bind himself contractually to serve an institution for a term of years or even for life, although 'outside' work was still a possibility. For example, Richard Beke, a mason, had in 1435 been appointed master of the works at Canterbury Cathedral for life, but three years later the Mayor of London wrote to the Prior of Canterbury asking that Beke should be allowed to inspect London Bridge and advise on its preservation. Earlier in his career, Beke had been chief mason for the bridge, and his knowledge of its fabric was naturally still of great value.

The greatest patron of all was the Crown. Some craftsmen — principally masons and carpenters — were virtually pressganged into its service, but for most people service to the Crown was an ideal to be aimed at. The king's palaces and castles all needed constant maintenance, but the attraction of royal service lay in new projects and in the high level of capability required. In every generation, the best craftsmen were often working for the Crown, whether on the basis of a contract of employment, like most masons, carvers, carpenters and painters, or on the basis of specific commissions, like goldsmiths, embroiderers, stationers (booksellers) or limners (book illustrators). The king and the members of his court spread their orders widely, usually preferring to engage a range of people rather than become dependent on one man and his workshop. The most famous mason of medieval England, and the only one of whom a full-length biography has been written, Henry Yevele (d. 1400), spent much of his life in and out of the service of Edward III and Richard II. He also worked for the London Charterhouse, Canterbury Cathedral, the Black Prince, John of Gaunt, St Alban's Abbey, the City of London, John, Lord Cobham, William of Wykeham, Bishop of Winchester and St Paul's Cathedral — a roll-call of most of the principal patrons of the day. Cross-fertilization of ideas resulted from the consequent travels around the country, to the benefit of both Yevele's and the nation's artistic development: Yevele was able to put into practice with one patron what he had experimented with for another, while he acted as a channel or focus by which the latest court style was brought to the provinces.

As the court was constantly giving work to craftsmen who had come from the provinces, so its fashions and style, albeit in a modified or watered-down form, would be brought back to other parts of the realm. The movement of ideas was not entirely one way, however; the Perpendicular style of architecture is now generally recognized as having its origins in the 'Kentish tracery' first found in and around Canterbury in the 1290s. It was brought into the contemporary court style by such Kentish master masons as Michael of Canterbury (*fl.* 1275–1321), the original architect of St Stephen's Chapel at Westminster.

The Gothic style was one that can almost be said to have depended on drawings. Once an architectural design for ground plans, elevations or cross-sections had been rendered as a drawing, it could be used as an all-purpose model serving craftsmen in other kinds of activity. Most medieval craftsmen worked in only one medium, and the polymath who could turn his hand to designing a textile as well as a building or a stained glass window was as rare then as he is now, but a single drawing could be used by different sorts of craftsmen, perhaps over several generations. The Pepysian Sketchbook at Magdalene College, Cambridge, is the only major group of medieval English designs to survive, and perfectly exemplifies this practice. It is not so much a book as a bound collection of sheets, with drawings that were made over a period of four or five generations, from the later fourteenth to the late fifteenth century. It contains three architectural drawings (two for moulding profiles, or cross-sections, and one for tracery), two drawings that seem to be textile patterns, and a series of painted, shaded and outline drawings, made at different dates, of single figures and of birds and animals. Some of the animal pictures seem to be derived from earlier models, perhaps as early as the 1320s, but others give the appearance of having been taken from life, and thus look forward to Renaissance practice.

It is tantalizing that the medieval history of the Pepysian collection will never be known — who owned it, and how far other people were given access to it, at different times. Yet it would be a mistake to see too much of a dichotomy of interests between the different sorts of craftsmen who may have benefited from using it. The very specialization that was so characteristic of the medieval craftsman also meant that he was accustomed to collaborate with those who practised in media different from his own. Only in the most general of ways would an architect concern himself with the decoration of what he had designed, since an architect was simply a mason (or possibly a carpenter) with a knowledge of geometry and an ability to draw, and his principal role was generally as executant of the buildings that he had designed. A master mason would not tell a master carpenter how to design or set about his work, or vice versa; every master craftsman was supreme in his own sphere. Accordingly, a structure with a timber roof would be likely to be the design of two men — a mason and a carpenter working in collaboration, as Henry Yevele and the carpenter Hugh Herland must have done when they designed the walls and roof of Westminster Hall in the 1390s. The hall's stained glass was the work of the king's glazier, William Burgh, who must have collaborated with both Herland (who had been made controller of the works for this major building project) as well as the specially appointed royal Clerk of the Works. The clear demarcation lines between all the principal craftsmen's particular roles would have made them free from rivalry or interference with each other's individual skills, and they would therefore have had nothing to lose by sharing their model drawings with each other.

Another factor that might have encouraged the owner of the Pepysian drawings to lend them would have been the fact that only the architectural drawings would have been regarded as designs that were personal to their creator and therefore professional 'secrets'. The drawings of birds and animals would have been seen for what they were — motifs drawn from the stock furnished by tradition and personal observation; they were not designs for actual objects or works of art. Motifs might enjoy a wide currency, lasting for centuries, and even the principal elements of a design might be popular throughout Europe. The mid- to late fourteenth-century swan mazer or drinking bowl at Corpus Christi College, Cambridge, which has a trick mechanism to siphon its contents into the lap of the unwary, is very close in design to a cup illustrated in the sketchbook of the thirteenth-century French architect, Villard de Honnecourt — and it is possible that Villard's drawing may itself hark back to an earlier sketch. The original purchaser of the Corpus Christi College mazer would have bought it because he was amused by it and because it had been well made, not because he wished to acquire something of an original conception. An unusual design was certainly valued if well made, but the medieval aesthetic was one that looked primarily for skill in craftsmanship and for colour, richness and even for value of materials.

Uncertainty as to the extent of English artistic originality has often been raised in the last century or two by those who have studied such medieval works of art as survive in England. The anonymity of virtually all medieval works of art (other than architectural works whose master masons may be named in contemporary financial or administrative documents) has combined with a modern inferiority complex about the talent of medieval English craftsmen. The result has been the view that the finest works of art surviving from Gothic England must be attributable to foreign-born artists. Thus, it has been argued or, worse still, assumed that both the Westminster Abbey retable (c. 1270s) and the Wilton Diptych portrait of Richard II (c. 1390s) are French.

There was much in the Gothic style that transcended the style of any particular country. But English art, like that of any other European country, had strengths that enabled it to absorb and anglicize a foreign style. Neither art nor its practitioners were constrained by any regnal boundaries, and leading craftsmen — especially masons and sculpters, who expected to travel from one job to another — commonly worked in more than one country. For the design and supervision of the building of Conway, Caernarfon, Harlech and other castles in North Wales, Edward I relied chiefly on James of St George, a master mason who came from Savoy. The castles have a number of unmistakably English features, and yet they display some patently foreign traces, such as the polygonal towers and bands of differently coloured stone at Caernarfon of which the only known precedent are the walls built round Constantinople by the Emperor

Theodosius. Nevertheless, England's artistic relations with Savoy can also be said to have been a two-way affair: early in the fourteenth century, Count Amadeus V of Savoy was travelling in Europe and while in London chose to buy not only two panel paintings, showing the allegory of the Three Living and the Three Dead, but also a secret (or personal) seal and chain of gold.

The extreme destructiveness of the English Reformation and the iconoclasm of the mid-seventeenth century have left only a tragically small number of medieval works of art in England, although parish churches and cathedrals and other buildings of stone have survived quite well. This loss is the more unfortunate because England's strength may have been in the making of small-sized objects rather than in architecture or architectural sculpture. Before the Norman Conquest, England was celebrated for its embroidery and for the work of its goldsmiths and it may have continued to excel in these and other crafts that depended on the craftsman's technical skills. This was recognized in the term applied to French master masons' work, *opus francigenum*, which was matched by *opus anglicanum*, English work, for English embroidery. Much of the extant medieval English embroidery is to be found in continental churches or museums, which testifies to how much it was valued by continental patrons in the Middle Ages. English memorial brasses of the fourteenth century — their earliest period — often show an exquisite mastery of line drawing, but they were so much an English phenomenon that they cannot fairly be compared with the few surviving continental brasses. No medieval English gold or silver shrines survive, but there are still sufficient English seal impressions for it to be possible to assert that Amadeus V's confidence in the ability of English goldsmiths was in no way misplaced. The best English thirteenth- or fourteenth-century seals were of superlative quality and show a mastery of craftsmanship that fully matched the work of continental goldsmiths.

England in the Middle Ages was more closely assimilated into continental culture than it has been, for example, over the last hundred years. Linguistic differences were over-ridden by the common use of Latin. For most of the Middle Ages, England's rulers regarded themselves as lords of at least a major part of France. It is true that Parisian culture was often looked up to and imitated or purchased by English monarchs and courtiers, but the overall effect of all this on English craftsmen must have been highly beneficial: they escaped the perils of insularity, and they enjoyed the benefits of a far wider market for their products.

V THE ARCHITECTURAL SETTING OF GOTHIC ART

Peter Draper

THE ARCHITECTURAL LEGACY OF THE MIDDLE AGES is familiar to us through the splendour of the cathedrals and the numerous parish churches that are still in use or through monuments that are known only as evocative ruins — slighted castles and destroyed monasteries. Yet even when these monuments survive relatively intact, it is often not appreciated just how much the original appearance has been altered and therefore how much of the original meaning has also been lost, particularly when essential interior furnishings and decoration are lacking.

Architecture is a demonstrative art, and the power to impress and to convey meaning is an essential part of its function. Social, political, economic and spiritual aspirations can be expressed in architecture and it is in this vital respect that architecture differs from building. Even those parts of a building which seem purely functional may have symbolic value, and the two aspects can rarely be separated. The scale and pretension of the architecture of churches can be equally expressive of political power as of religious aspiration. The physical fabric of churches, from the grandest cathedral to the simplest parish church, is also a very tangible manifestation and an ever-present reminder of the hierarchical, increasingly centralized institution of the Church and of its dominant role in medieval society.

To make the most of the evidence which these buildings can afford, we need to interpret the architecture in a variety of ways and, above all, to keep in mind the vital interrelationship between architecture and the other arts. For, in addition to possessing its own symbolic value, architecture was informed and enriched by sculpture, paintings and painted decoration, tapestries and stained glass, as well as providing the setting for the use of metalwork and manuscript illumination. In turn, the formal and symbolic

Caernarfon Castle. The distinctive polygonal towers and the bands of different-coloured masonry consciously recall the Theodosian walls of Constantinople evoking the imperial associations of a site where, in 1283, was discovered the supposed body of Magnus Maximus, the father of the Emperor Constantine.

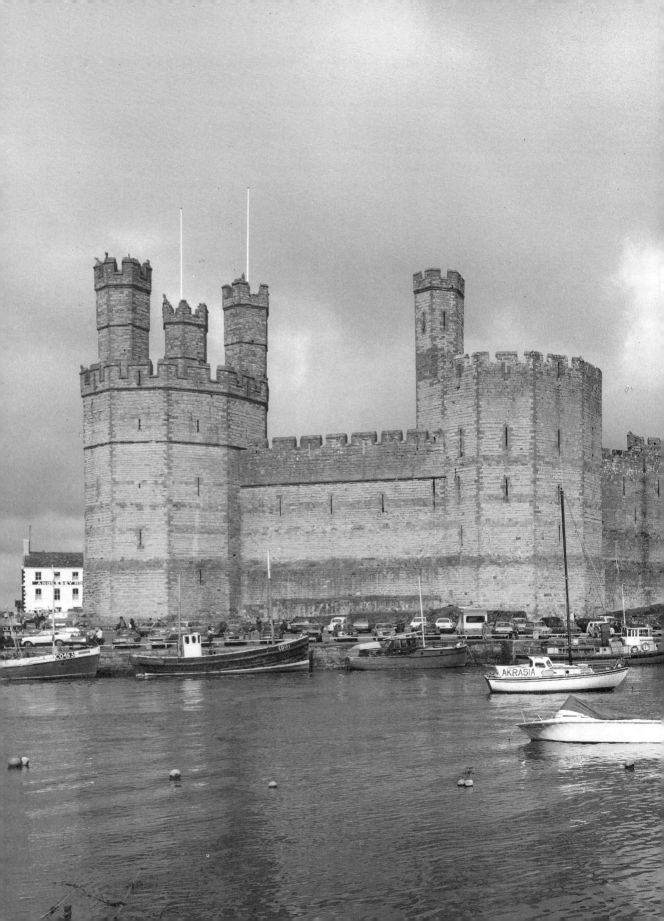

vocabulary employed in these other arts owed much to the forms of the surrounding architecture. The colourful splendour of churches depended on the furnishings, and it was the total effect which served as such a powerful metaphorical evocation of the Heavenly Jerusalem as described in Revelations xxi.10–27.

A comparable symbolic interpretation may also be applied to secular architecture. The majority of fortified structures, for example, ranging from the grandest castles to fortified manor-houses, were primarily demonstrative. Walls and towers were capable of serving a defensive purpose, but only the strongest castles built in the Middle Ages would have been able to withstand a determined siege. Even with this type of building, where it might be expected that the creation of a defensible stronghold would be the primary purpose and that the architecture would be determined predominantly by military considerations, the towers and gatehouses were also intended to be symbolic and, in order to be understood, castles need to be seen within the context of the feudal hierarchy.

At the top of the scale, the magnificent series of castles built by Edward I to secure his conquest of Wales provide interesting examples of the balance struck between military considerations such as firing lines, formal considerations such as the desirability of symmetry, as at Beaumaris, and symbolism, as in the conscious evocation of the Theodosian walls of Constantinople by the use of coloured banding in the walls of Caernarfon. Castles, like armour and heraldry, could also reflect chivalric ideals: evocatively, in the fantastic silhouettes created by innumerable turrets or, more specifically, in the Round Table at Winchester. To a lesser degree this approach also applied to manor-houses. When a landowner built a fortified manor or castle, the building had not only to accommodate his household, which could be quite extensive, and to provide an appropriate setting for the performance of his public duties, but also the architecture itself had to have a degree of pretension carefully attuned to the position of that landowner in the social hierarchy. The building of one or more towers on a manor-house may have afforded some means of defence against a small-scale attack or riot, but the number and size of the towers were more significant as a reflection of feudal status, of the owner's relationship with his superior lord. When a rich wool merchant purchased Stokesay in Shropshire in 1281, he built alongside the hall an impressive polygonal tower, obviously modelled on recent work at Caernarfon, in order to assert his new social status. At the same time, Robert Burnell, chancellor and Bishop of Bath and Wells, built a substantial house at Acton Burnell, also in Shropshire, with four imposing corner towers; but with large traceried windows on the ground

Westminster Hall (1097–9; remodelled 1394–1401). The outer walls belong to the aisled hall built by William Rufus, but the spectacular timber roof by Richard II's master carpenter, Hugh Herland, is evidence of the richness possible in secular buildings that so rarely survive. The use of hammer-beams enabled the hall to be roofed in a single span.

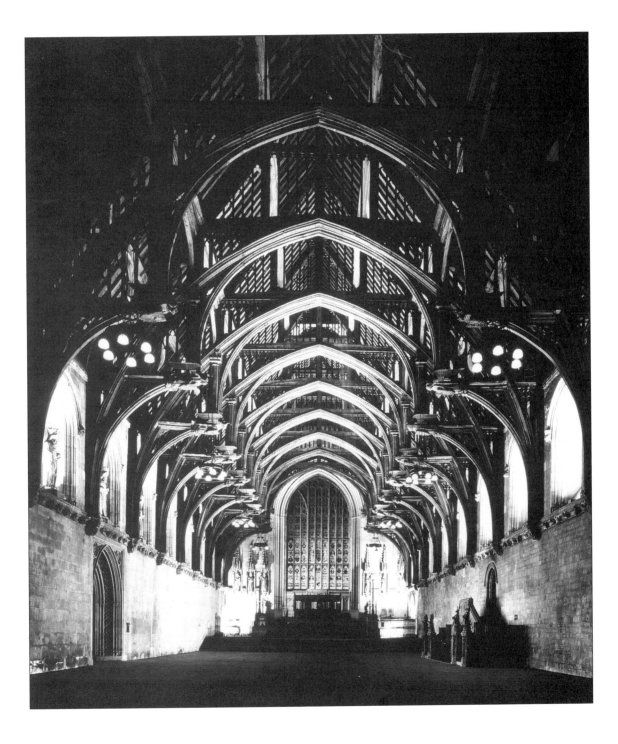

floor this house can never have been seriously defensible and it is interesting that Burnell was to employ similar architectural forms at his episcopal palace in the more peaceful surroundings at Wells.

External appearance was important in all these houses, but the sense of grandeur was also expressed in the interior, mainly in the Great Hall, which served a variety of public functions. The grandest of these halls were aisled, some having stone or marble piers as at Oakham Castle, Henry III's hall at Winchester and Archbishop Langton's hall at Canterbury. Many of them also had impressively elaborate timber roofs, splendid tiled floors and from the late thirteenth century magnificent traceried windows. Unfortunately, few remaining secular buildings from the Middle Ages retain their original decoration or fittings. The survival rate of secular works of art tends to be much lower than for religious works as they are more susceptible to changes of political fortune and to the vagaries of fashion. Moreover, it is important to remember that secular patrons spent considerable sums on clothes, armour, plate, jewellery and manuscripts as well as on the temporary but often very elaborate staging of feasts and tournaments and these, too, would have formed an essential part of the experience of architecture.

Large-scale architectural complexes were almost always surrounded by walls and entered through gatehouses. Many towns have substantial parts of their medieval walls and gates surviving — particularly good examples are still to be found at York and Chester — but cathedrals and monasteries were also enclosed in the same way. The walls and gatehouses of the Close at Salisbury survive almost intact and numerous examples of impressive monastic gatehouses are to be found all over the country, notably at Kirkham Priory in Yorkshire, Bury St Edmunds in Suffolk and St Augustine's, Canterbury. The symbolic importance of these walls is reflected in their prominent representation on the seals of towns and cities.

The architecture of the churches themselves was certainly demonstrative in the sense that in size and degree of elaboration it usually extended far beyond the strict and essential requirements for the performance of the liturgy. This is particularly true of 'great churches' — cathedrals, collegiate and monastic churches, where the sense of scale could be greatly enhanced by towers and spires and the pinnacled or crenellated profile of the exterior — but it might also be true of lesser buildings. The replacement in stone of the often modest Anglo-Saxon parish churches by the Normans was a powerful assertion of the new political order. In trying to understand the way in which churches developed, we must take account of more than just the changing architectural vocabulary (or style) that was employed by successive generations; we must try to be aware of the many varied factors

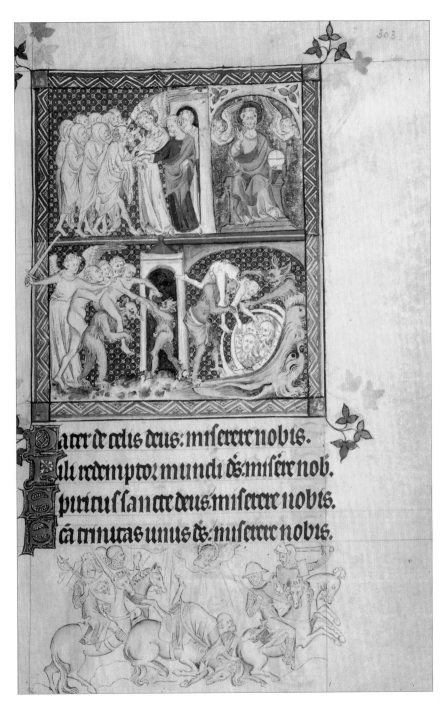

1 *Queen Mary Psalter,*
early fourteenth century:
a folio from a manuscript
in which women appear
so prominently as to
suggest that the volume
was commissioned by
a high-born lady,
perhaps Isabella,
queen of Edward II.

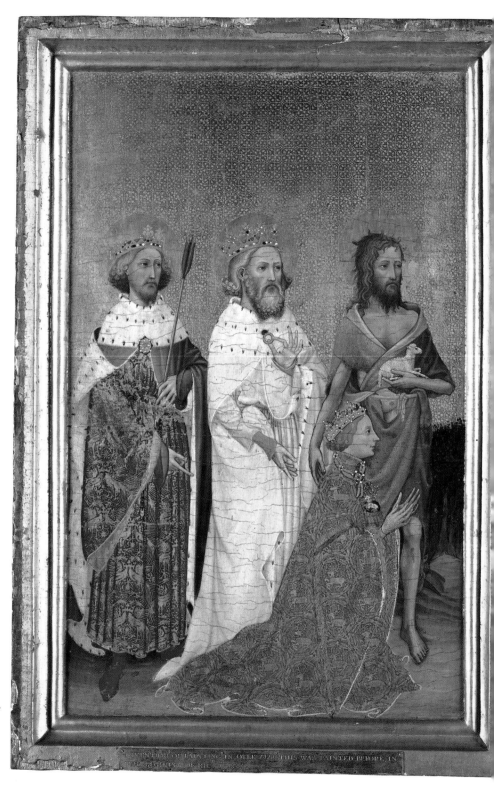

2 Sacred sponsorship: Edmund, king and martyr, Edward the Confessor and John the Baptist present Richard II to the Virgin and Child and their attendant angels, badged in the young king's livery in the Wilton Diptych.

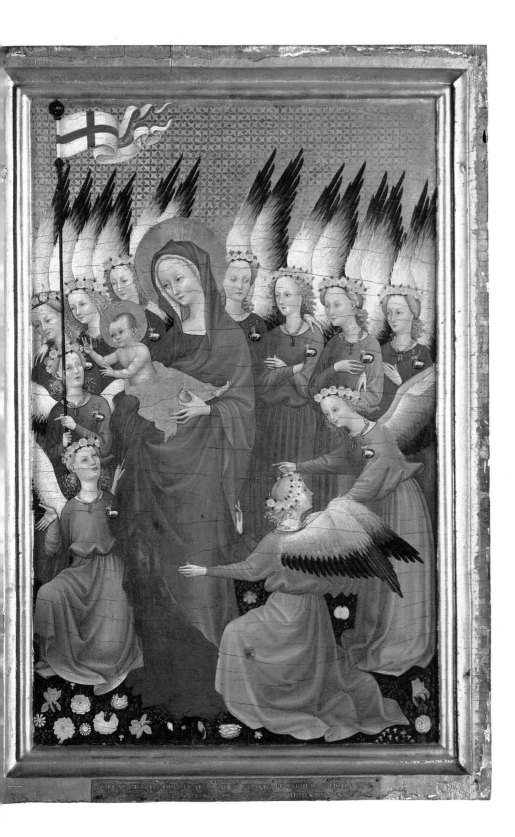

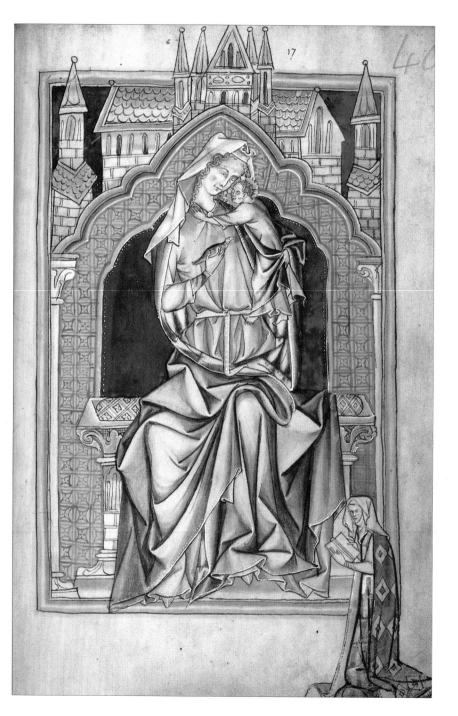

3 (Right) *Donor portrait from the Lambeth Apocalypse of Lady Eleanor de Quincy kneeling before the Virgin and Child.*

4 (Opposite) *The Old Testament Israelite hero David (whose coronation is illustrated in the Glazier Psalter) was one of the 'types' of Christian kingship, including that of Arthur, to which English monarchs looked.*

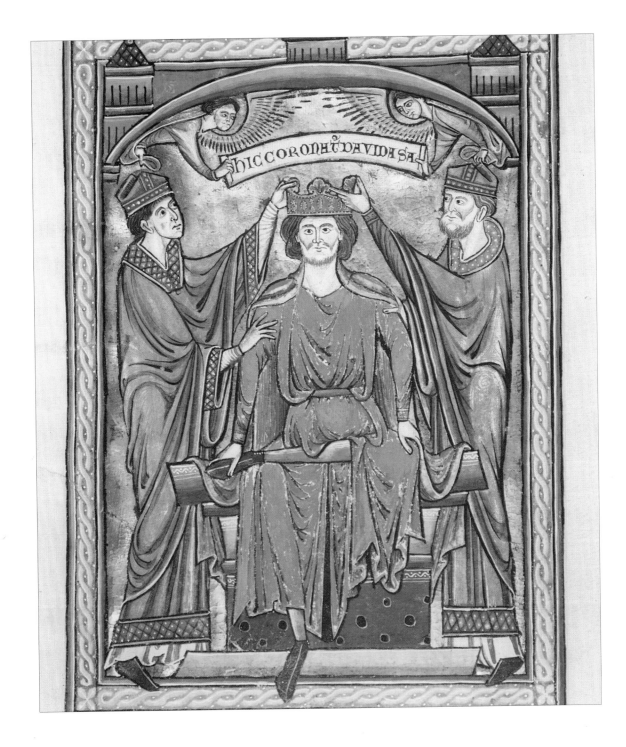

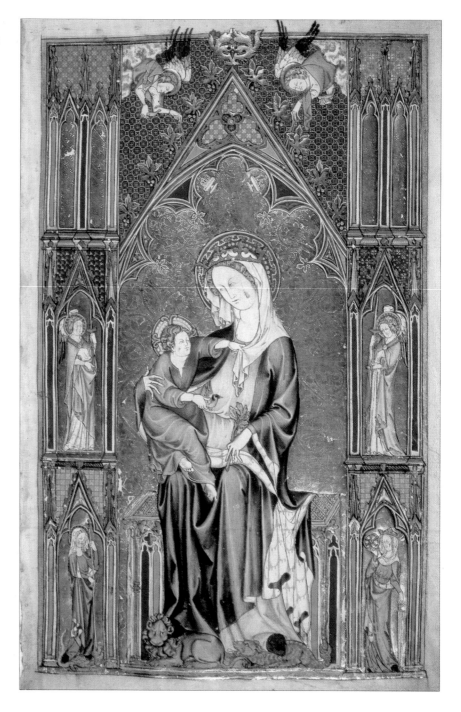

5 *The Virgin and Child, an illuminated page from the de Lisle Psalter (c. 1310), given in 1339 by Lord de Lisle to his daughters Audere and Alborou.*

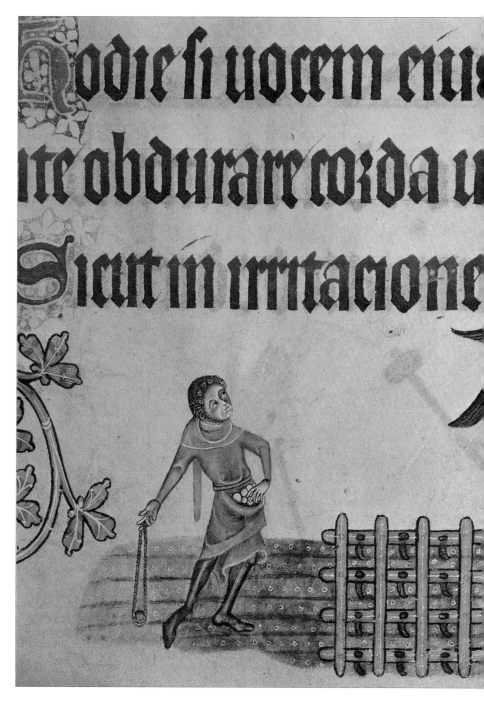

9 Harrowing, a marginal scene from the psalter written and illuminated for Sir Geoffrey Luttrell, of Irnham in Lincolnshire, early in the fourteenth century.

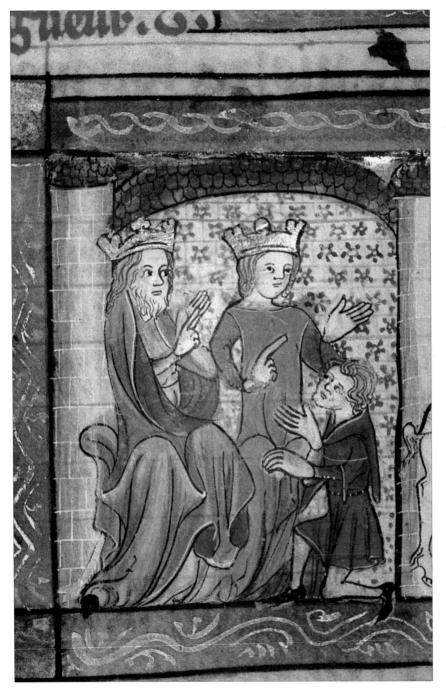

8 Gawain, perhaps the most exacting model of Christian knighthood in Arthurian romance, takes leave of the king and Guinevere (French fourteenth-century manuscript).

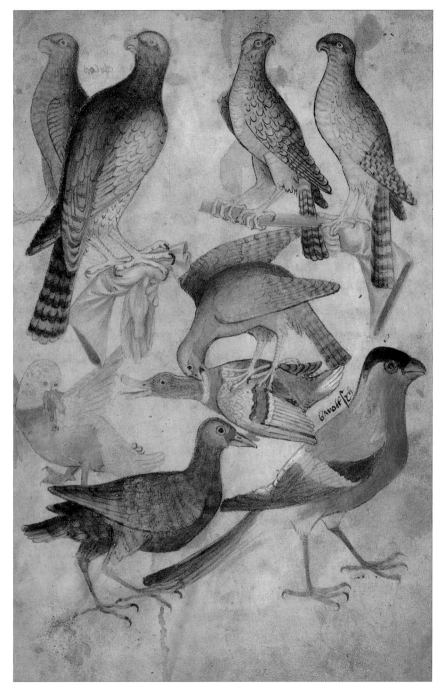

7 Hawks, mallard ducks, a bullfinch and other birds, from the Pepysian Sketchbook (late fourteenth century).

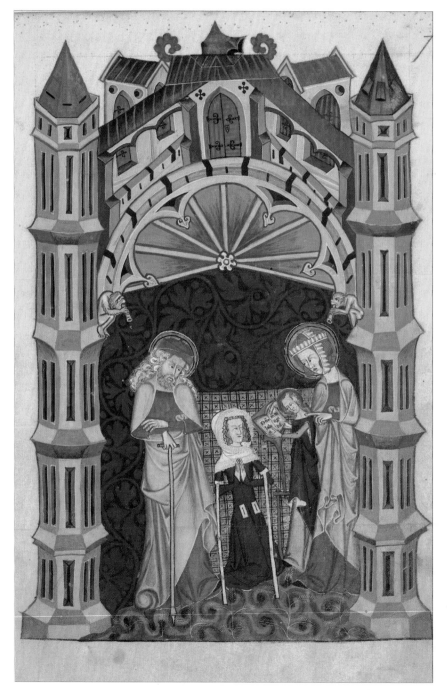

6 Illustration from the
Fitzwarin Psalter showing
the female donor kneeling
in front of St Anne as she
is teaching her daughter,
the Virgin Mary, to read.

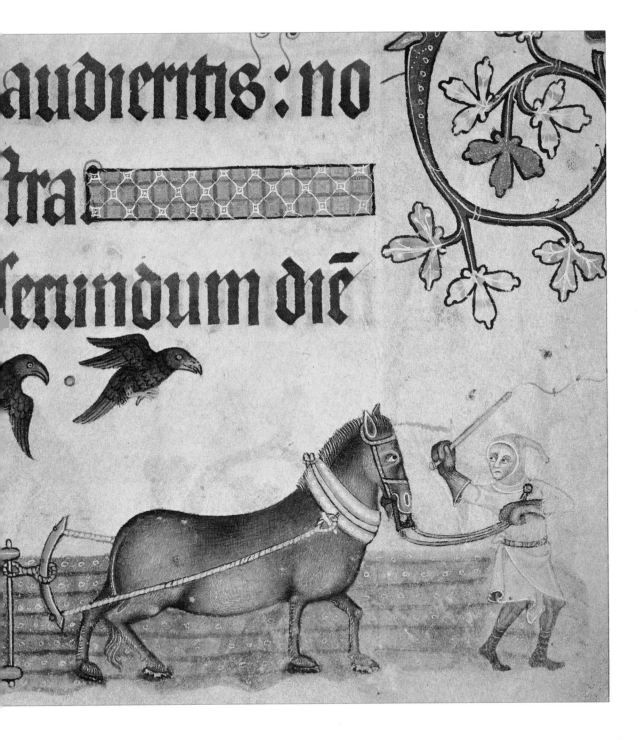

audientis : no
tra
secundum die

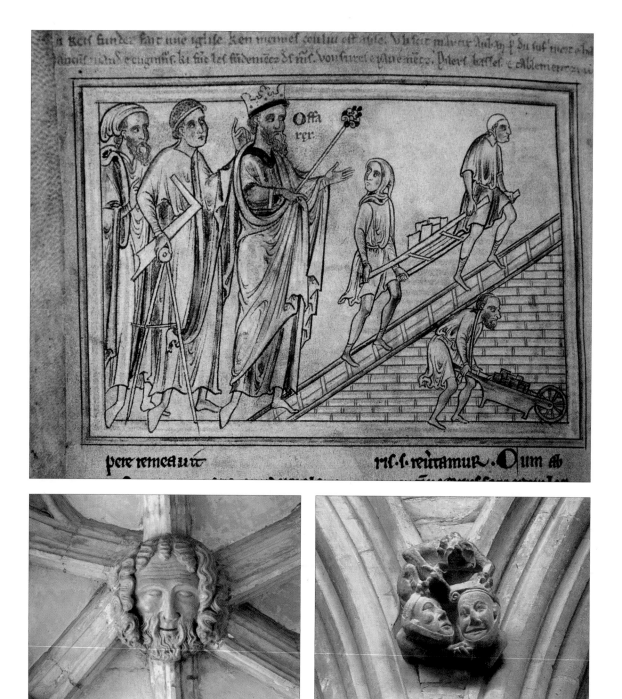

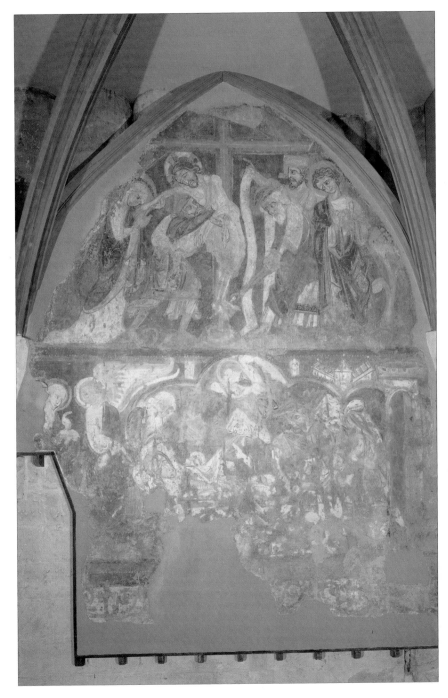

10 (Opposite, above) *King Offa directing the building of St Albans Church. From Matthew Paris's life of St Alban, written at St Albans Abbey, c. 1240.*

11 (Opposite, below left) *Supposed portrait of the architect Henry Yevele (d. 1400); it has the appearance of having been taken from a death mask. Stone boss in the east walk of Canterbury Cathedral cloister; early fifteenth century.*

12 (Opposite, below right) *Tutivillus and the gossips: corbel from south nave arcade, St Denis, Sleaford, Lincolnshire.*

13 (Left) *The Deposition from the cycle of Entombment and Resurrection paintings, c. 1220, in the Holy Sepulchre Chapel, Winchester Cathedral.*

parole de la passiun nostre seignur e signifie la crux ihu crist. Mes cel
serrum de boues.

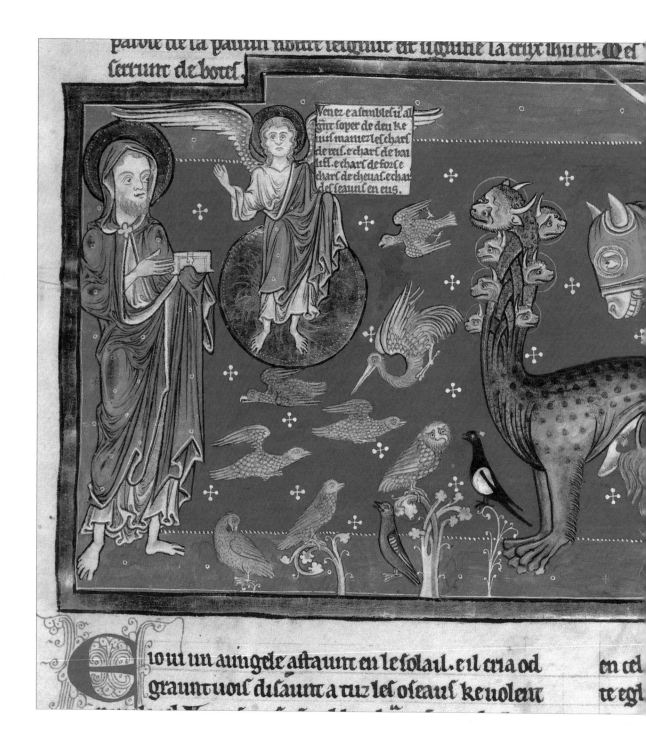

Venez e asembletz uuſ al
gint soper de deu ke
uuſ manietz les chars
de reis. e chars de bai
liſs. e chars de force
chars de cheuaſ. e char
des seauns en eus.

Eio uit un aungele astaunt en le solail. e il cria od
graunt uoiſ disaunt a tuz les oseaus ke uolent

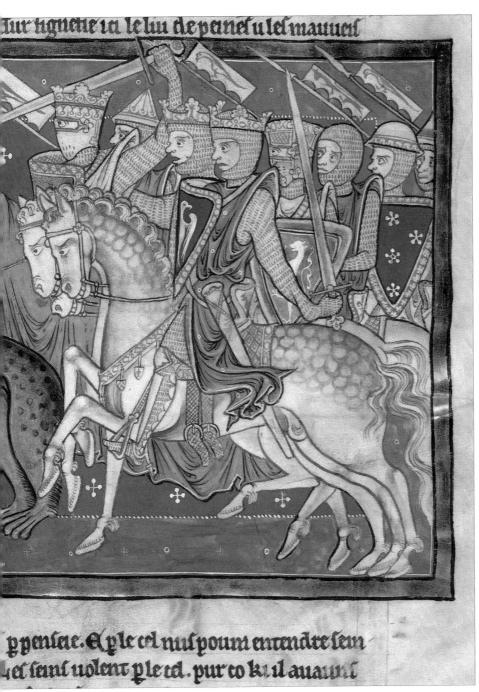

14 The last battle of good and evil — from an English-made apocalypse of the early thirteenth century. Contemporary military detail mingles with the mythical.

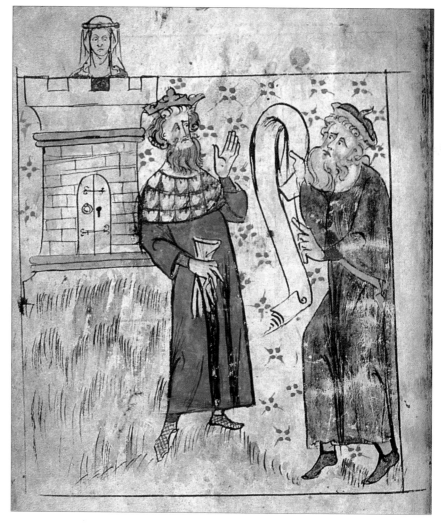

15 (Right) *Uther Pendragon, Arthur's father, confers with Merlin about his love for Ygerna, wife of Gorlois, Duke of Cornwall, who is pictured here in Tintagel Castle. Merlin transformed Uther into an exact likeness of Gorlois, in which form he fathered Arthur on Ygerna. (From Langtoft's 'Chronicle of England', reign of Edward II.)*

16 (Below) *The wall painting of the Crucifixion with Saint Mary and Saint John which forms the reredos behind the altar on the east wall of Brent Eleigh Church in Suffolk.*

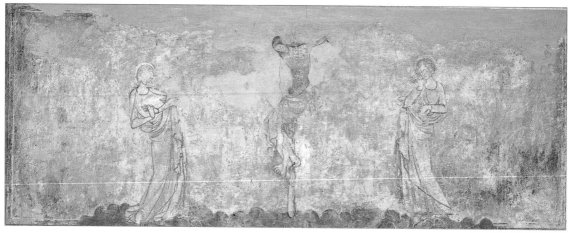

that determined the form of these highly complex buildings. Among these it was the performance of the liturgy that was the essential purpose of these buildings, and their architectural development should not be separated from the context of contemporary devotional practice.

Any attempt to correlate the changing forms of architecture with devotional practice is complicated by the widespread, sometimes wholesale, destruction of images and liturgical furnishings. This destruction started with the Reformation, continued through later waves of iconoclasm in the seventeenth century, followed by comparative neglect in the eighteenth century, and culminated in the extensive restorations of the nineteenth century. The cumulative effect, compounded by the vandalism of the twentieth century, has been to destroy much of the evidence of the medieval appearance of our churches. This appearance, however, was not the same throughout the medieval period. Between the twelfth and sixteenth centuries important changes also took place in liturgical and devotional practice, and these changes had a significant influence on the development of architecture.

The interweaving of some of the factors that inspired and motivated men to build in the Middle Ages can be followed in a résumé of the building histories of the rival metropolitan churches of York and Canterbury. On his arrival at Canterbury in 1070, the new Norman archbishop, Lanfranc, rebuilt the venerable Anglo-Saxon church on the model of the most recent churches in Normandy as a demonstrative gesture by the new regime; at York, the opportunity for Thomas of Bayeux to rebuild came with the burning of the Anglo-Saxon church by the Danes in 1075. Yet, before 1100, the Benedictine community at Canterbury had undertaken a substantial enlargement of the east end of their church, including an impressive crypt and two sets of towers flanking the choir. This eastward extension of the church, which became known as the 'glorious choir', enabled the screen dividing the choir from the nave to be moved from the nave to the east side of the main crossing, creating, in effect, a separate church where the community could perform the *Opus Dei* free from disturbance by the laity. In the 1150s, stirred by the example of Canterbury where he had been treasurer, the ambitious Archbishop of York, Roger of Pont l'Évêque, rebuilt the east end of the minster on a much grander scale, also with an extended crypt, tower-like structures flanking the high altar, and a substantial two-towered west front. This had scarcely been completed when Canterbury came decisively back into the limelight with the murder of Thomas Becket in 1170, followed by the disastrous fire of 1174 which provided the monks with a fortuitous opportunity to reconstruct yet again

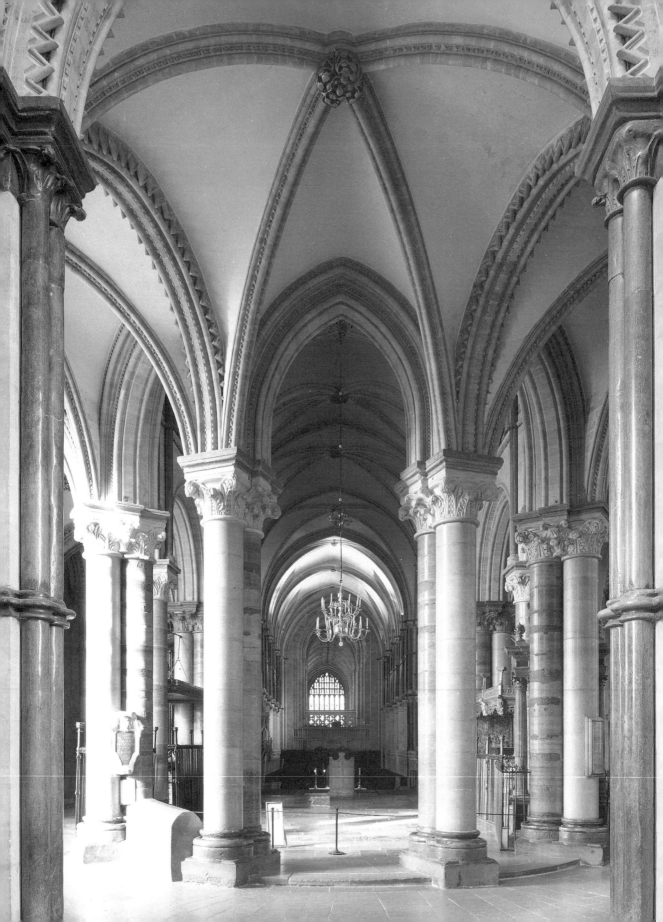

the eastern part of their church and to provide a sumptuous setting for the shrine of their recently martyred archbishop. His relics were finally translated to the new shrine in 1220 in a spectacular ceremony staged by Archbishop Stephen Langton.

The response at York by Archbishop Walter de Grey was to secure from the pope in 1226 the canonization of William Fitzherbert, a twelfth-century archbishop of York, and, in connection with the promotion of that cult, to rebuild the transepts of the church on a much larger scale, possibly with a view to a general reconstruction of the minster. This eventually took place in the early fourteenth century, beginning in 1291 with the rebuilding of the eleventh-century nave and the twelfth-century west front (the west window was glazed in 1339) and was followed by a full-scale rebuilding of the east end in order to provide suitably grand accommodation for the clergy east of the crossing, a chapel of appropriate size and richness within the main body of the church for the popular devotions to the Virgin and a suitably splendid setting for the refurbished shrine of the saint in keeping with the grandeur being accorded to other cults elsewhere. York now appeared a relatively homogeneous building with most of it having been rebuilt between *c.* 1280 and *c.* 1380. By this date, however, Canterbury still had its eleventh-century nave, which, though it was of less interest to the monks, must have looked decidedly old-fashioned. So a complete reconstruction on a suitably impressive scale was undertaken, including the west towers, though the north-west tower was not in fact rebuilt until the nineteenth century. During the course of the fifteenth century, York completed its rebuilding with three imposing towers, to which Canterbury responded in the early sixteenth century with the magnificent central tower known as Bell Harry.

A brief summary like this gives little indication of the strength of the motivation for embarking on successive building projects which generally took at least two generations to complete and often placed a severe strain on the resources of even the wealthiest of religious communities. Nor does it take into account the extensive work on the 'furnishings': the altars, the screens, the shrines and tombs which became ever more elaborate through the later Middle Ages.

Inspired to a considerable extent by the example of the two metropolitan churches, there was by the thirteenth century a widely accepted idea of the architectural vocabulary that was felt to be appropriate to churches of the highest status; a vocabulary that was distinctly insular and differed markedly from contemporary developments in France. This is particularly well illustrated by the rebuilding of the cathedral of Salisbury. In 1220 the cathedral was moved from the precincts of the castle at Old Sarum to a

Trinity Chapel, Canterbury Cathedral, looking west from the corona, showing the lavish setting of Purbeck and rich architectural detail which surrounded the shrine of St Thomas Becket.

virgin site near the river, hence the design was not determined by pre-existing buildings. The scale of the undertaking clearly demonstrated the importance of having an appropriately grand building to represent the status and authority of the bishop and to serve as the focal point of the diocese. The layout of the church and its associated buildings, on the other hand, reflects its primary function, that of making suitable provision for the ordered communal life of the canons who served the cathedral.

The cathedral was surrounded by houses for the canons and their deputies, the vicars choral, set within a walled close which could be locked at night. From the outset, a cloister was planned and by the end of the century the canons had been provided with an impressive chapter house, the splendour of which reflected the corporate prestige of the community. Within the church itself the eastern part was screened off for the almost exclusive use of the canons, the first three bays east of the main crossing being occupied by the stalls where the canons sat, or more often stood, for the many hours of services prescribed in the liturgical customs of the cathedral. Generous space beyond the eastern crossing was allowed for the elaborate ceremonial around the high altar. The two sets of transepts and the aisles of the choir accommodated twelve altars, all of which were conveniently accessible by a continuous procession path — an important consideration as they all had to be visited for the asperges in the Sunday procession during mass. The altar next in importance after the high altar was that of the eastern axial chapel, which was dedicated to the Trinity, but from the outset the altar was used for the daily sung Mass of the Virgin, a practice which had become widespread a few years earlier: a manifestation of the increasing importance attached to the cult of the Virgin.

It is possible that within this very spacious east end of the church provision was also made for the intended shrine of St Osmund. Such an arrangement had been made for St Swithun at Winchester shortly before this and when Osmund's relics were brought down from Old Sarum in 1226 a petition was made to the pope for his formal canonization. Osmund was but one of a number of indigenous bishops who were the focus of popular local cults; some were Anglo-Saxon and long-established, like St Etheldreda at Ely and St Wulfstan at Worcester, but others were recently deceased bishops such as St Hugh at Lincoln or William Bytton at Wells. Following the successful outcome of the petition on behalf of Edward the Confessor at Westminster in 1161, official canonization from the pope was sought for a number of these cults. Not all these petitions were successful and St Osmund had to wait until 1457 for his formal canonization. Some of these cults enjoyed wide popularity, while others remained localized, but their promotion and the pilgrims they attracted often provided the stimulus to rebuild the east end of the church in order to make suitable provision for the shrine.

Access to shrines provided one of the few occasions when the laity would have been allowed into the east end of the church. Confined for the most part to the nave, they would generally have entered the church through the elaborate north porch, not the west door. This would have been reserved primarily for the Sunday procession as it re-entered the church after it had passed around the cloister and paused for a station before the west front, which at Salisbury was designed, as at Wells, like a great screen. In the absence of west towers, the dominating vertical accent at Salisbury was provided by the central stone spire, the crowning glory of the cathedral, rising to a height of over 400 feet. This was the final stage in the building campaign and, as built, was certainly more ambitious than the crossing tower originally envisaged. It is likely that the entire cathedral was completed within a hundred years of its foundation and there is clearly a strong sense of continuity and consistency in the design which permits a confident assessment of the intended character of the architecture although, as the building progressed, fashionable new forms were introduced, such as the use of bar tracery in the cloisters and the windows of the chapter house.

To understand the distinctive qualities of Salisbury within its contemporary context, we need to remember that the foundation stone of Salisbury was laid within weeks of the spectacular translation of Becket's relics to his new shrine in 1220, and it is not surprising therefore that Salisbury shows some interesting similarities to Canterbury, although there are also significant differences. Canterbury had set new standards of splendour for cathedral architecture, but it was in some respects exceptional in that it was a metropolitan church set within a Benedictine monastery and the character of the rebuilding had been strongly influenced by the need to provide an impressive setting for the popular shrine of the recently martyred archbishop. Salisbury, on the other hand, had a chapter of secular canons, led in the late twelfth and early thirteenth century by Richard Poore, first as dean then as bishop. Poore, a leading ecclesiastic of the reform movement, devoted much of his considerable energy to regularizing the way of life of the canons and to codifying the liturgical customs — the way in which the services were conducted in the cathedral. The liturgical rites or customs of most cathedrals were broadly similar, though each had its own local and sometimes quite distinct variations in practice, particularly in the celebration of feast days associated with specific saints. Under Bishop Richard Poore, the customs at Salisbury were thoroughly revised, clarifying

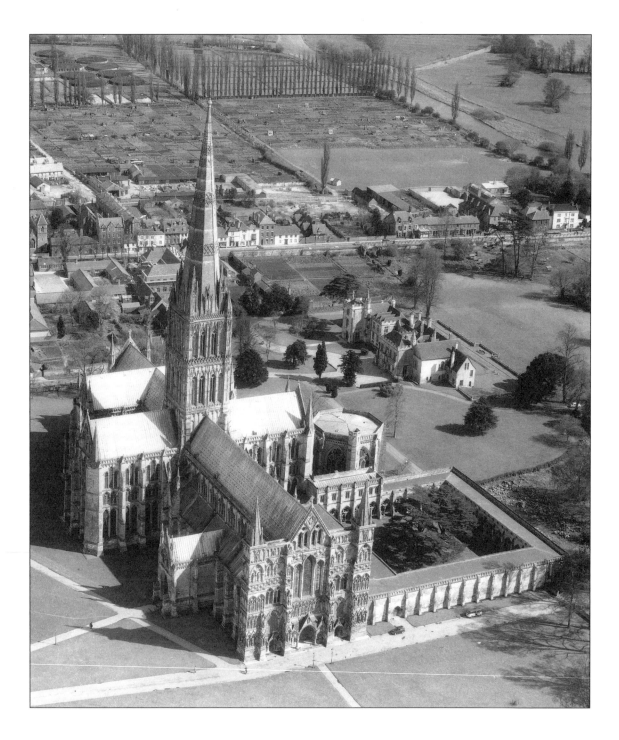

the strict order of precedence of all the feasts and specifying precisely the order of service for every occasion. These customs were also designed to be employed, in so far as they were applicable, in parish churches as well as in the larger collegiate churches of the diocese. So successful was this codification at Salisbury that, by the end of the Middle Ages, almost all the cathedrals and dioceses in England had adopted the Use of Sarum.

The significance of these reformed customs for the architectural design of Salisbury lies in the fact that although much of the rich vocabulary of Canterbury was used — notably the complexity of the pier forms, the embellishment of the mouldings and the lavish use of Purbeck marble — it was, appropriately, employed in a more restrained and almost chaste manner, in keeping with the elaborate but orderly character of the liturgical customs. This sense of decorum in medieval architecture, of suiting the architecture to the particular function or status of the building, is seen most clearly at one extreme in the austerity of early Cistercian architecture and at the other in the sumptuous and scintillating decoration of the settings of shrines, as for example at Canterbury — an almost literal as well as metaphorical evocation of the Heavenly Jerusalem. Between these extremes, it is not always easy to discern the subtleties of differentiation because the successive changes and restorations of all our major monuments mean that we cannot avoid seeing them through the eyes of preceding generations, especially those of the nineteenth century. This can dull our sensitivity to this sense of decorum in the original work and at worst may result in the grave distortion of our understanding. At Salisbury, the extensive restoration by Wyatt in the late eighteenth century has tended to obscure the subtle but significant differentiation between nave and choir, formerly accentuated by the substantial stone pulpitum. This separation is clearly signalled in the design where the variety and comparative richness of the architecture of the choir and presbytery contrast with the simplified and uniform architecture of the nave.

Like the greater churches, the more modest parish churches also reflect these wider political and liturgical changes. In the early thirteenth century, the rebuilding in the fashionable new Early English style of a significant number of chancels, the part of the church which was the responsibility of the rector, can be seen as part of the contemporary reforms of the institution of the Church, as expressed in the statutes of the Fourth Lateran Council of 1215. Responsibility for the nave rested with the parishioners — and significantly this was often rebuilt in the later Middle Ages, sometimes on a much grander scale than the chancel, indicating the greater wealth available to an increasing number of lay patrons at that time. The great

Salisbury Cathedral, aerial view from the south-west. The cathedral, which dominates the town that grew up around it, was first and foremost the church of a community of canons and their vicars who lived in houses within the close, a walled and gated enclosure. Their daily life centred around the church, the chapter house and the cloister.

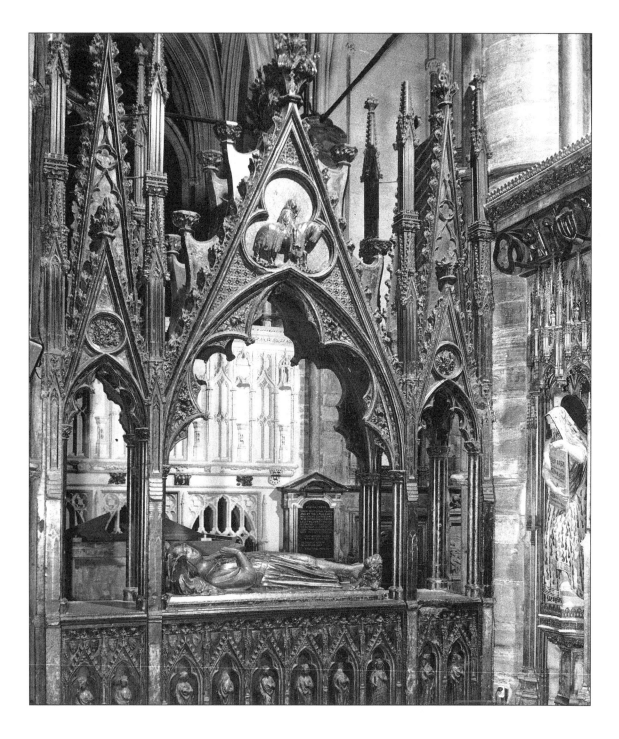

majority of the laity had only a distant relationship with the cathedral; the primary involvement was with the parish church where most people were baptized, married, confessed and buried. This involvement extended to the building and furnishing of churches and could take many forms. As a demonstration of 'good works', lay patrons might donate individual items necessary for the performance of the mass, such as chalices or service books, or be responsible for providing wall paintings or stained glass in which the donor was often clearly represented or identified by means of heraldry.

Tombs are perhaps the most obvious aspect of individual lay patronage and from the thirteenth century increasingly adopted the formal vocabulary of architecture together with its symbolic associations, as in the canopied tomb such as that of Archbishop Walter de Grey at York or Edmund Crouchback's tomb at Westminster Abbey. The latter tomb retains most of its original paint and shows, not only how richly colourful these furnishings could be, but also how much of the architectural vocabulary was repeated and elaborated in the painted decoration. Tombs might also form part of a chantry chapel. From the thirteenth century, the founding of chantries became increasingly popular through the later Middle Ages until such foundations were suppressed in 1547. Strictly speaking, the chantry was an endowment, usually in the form of rent from land, to pay for the services of a priest to celebrate the Mass of the Dead, normally for the souls of the donor and his family, although some chantries were founded by lay folk acting together in corporate bodies such as gilds and confraternities. The chantry could be established at an existing altar, but it often involved the construction of a new altar, or even a new chapel, which might be within or adjacent to the cathedral or parish church, and which might also accommodate the family tombs. The Beauchamp Chapel at Warwick is one of the grandest of these funerary chantry chapels.

As with other altars, these chantries had to be provided with the vestments, books and liturgical vessels necessary for the performance of the mass and such objects, associated with public devotional practice, account for a substantial proportion of the surviving works of medieval art. Given their use within an architectural context, it is perhaps not surprising that we find such extensive use of the formal vocabulary of architecture in painting, sculpture and in the so-called decorative arts. The most obvious example of a motif common to different art forms is that of the canopied niche, used either as an independent feature or arranged as a series to form arcading. Although this containing or framing feature is architectural in origin, a stage in its development seems to have taken place in metalwork; and with the 'precious' connotations that metalwork would have implied, it seems to

The tomb of Edmund Crouchback (d. 1296) in Westminster Abbey. This magnificent ciborium tomb is notable for the rich array of architectural features, showing the very close interrelationship between architecture and furnishings at this period. The rare survival of its complete painted decoration reminds us how much colour we have lost from medieval buildings.

have been given renewed importance and significance in architecture, particularly during the early fourteenth century. A striking example may be seen in the Lady Chapel at Ely, where the canopied niche is the leitmotiv of the surviving architecture, but would originally have been even more conspicuous as the dominating feature of the stained glass, where the figures in each light were surmounted by elaborate canopies, depicted as if three-dimensional. The same motif would almost certainly have formed the architectural frame of the painted altarpiece and quite possibly would have been used on an embroidered altar frontal, since it was also commonly found on vestments such as copes as a framing device for figurative scenes.

So common was the use of this architectural feature and so close was the interrelationship between the arts in the 'Decorated' period, that fashionable developments were very rapidly disseminated through different kinds of objects in a wide range of media: in stone and wrought-iron screens; in canopied tombs; in the elaborate wooden canopies of stalls and thrones; in embroidered textiles such as *opus anglicanum*; in painting and stained glass; and in the decoration of illuminated manuscripts, especially from East Anglia. The canopied niche was, however, more than just a framing device. It is likely that its symbolic significance, representing in microcosm the embracing architecture of the Church, the New Jerusalem, was carried back into full-scale buildings to reinforce the connotations of the familiar vocabulary of architecture. In the late twelfth century, the monk Gervase at Canterbury had used the term 'ciborium' (normally used for a canopy over a relic or altar) to describe the compartments of the rib-vaulted bays of the new work, and this association was surely still present in the splendid late medieval fan vaults.

These examples should serve as a timely reminder that our overriding concern with the formal vocabulary of architecture and its definition into stylistic categories would have meant little to the Middle Ages. Certainly, there would have been an awareness of new modes and of changing fashions, but not just in the enclosing architectural framework which for the most part is what survives today. There would have been a much greater interest in the iconography, and in the overall effect, including the furnishings. For all the richness of the elaborate canopied arcading in the Lady Chapel at Ely, the present clear, cold appearance belies the original enveloping warmth of colour of the polychrome and the stained glass. Far more serious, however, is the loss of so much of the wealth of figure sculpture from this chapel, which included more than a hundred scenes of the life of the Virgin, in addition to life-size figures on the walls. Not only does this deny us any semblance of the original aesthetic experience, but, more importantly, it obscures the elaborate iconographic programme, the very meaning of the building. Fragments of sculpture or stained glass out of context have only limited meaning; by the same token, architecture is immeasurably impoverished without the integral contribution of the other arts. In the consecration service, the Church is explicitly referred to as the New Jerusalem and it is this metaphorical interpretation of churches that we should keep constantly before us when considering that vital and fruitful interrelationship between the arts of the Middle Ages and their architectural setting.

VI DEVOTIONS AND DELIGHTS
The Illuminated Books of Gothic England

Janet Backhouse

VITAL TO OUR VIEW OF THE MIDDLE AGES are the illuminated manuscripts which have survived all hazards to become star attractions in the museums and libraries of the present day. Curators and exhibition organizers are well aware of the fascination which they exert over the general public, who relate to their intimate scale and jewel-like brilliance more readily than to the larger but often more fragmentary stone or metalwork of similar age. Popular first-hand knowledge of these treasures is inevitably limited to the single exhibited page or to the subject picked out for reproduction. Even in scholarly circles, manuscript studies were until comparatively recently regarded as somewhat esoteric. As each individual manuscript may contain dozens, in some cases even hundreds, of separate miniatures, this is one field in which exciting discoveries can still be made. Indeed, even the most famous and apparently thoroughly investigated manuscripts often manage to produce surprises when re-examined in the light of fresh developments elsewhere.

It is important never to lose sight of the fact that illuminated books were made by people and for people. Their miniatures are not independent works of divine inspiration, but illustrations relevant to the written text of the particular book in which they appear. To produce them cost money — often a very great deal of money — and if someone, somewhere, had not been prepared to pay the price, the manuscript would not have come into existence. During the early Middle Ages, the majority of the great masterpieces of illumination appeared in the context of copies of the Gospels or in grand liturgical manuscripts designed as accessories to public worship in a largely illiterate age. During the twelfth century, the emphasis shifted to large-scale bibles, saints' lives and martyrologies, all types of book which were liable to be read aloud during the daily cycle of life in a religious

Your humble servant; the artist Matthew Paris adoring the Virgin and Child in the frontispiece to his Historia Anglorum.

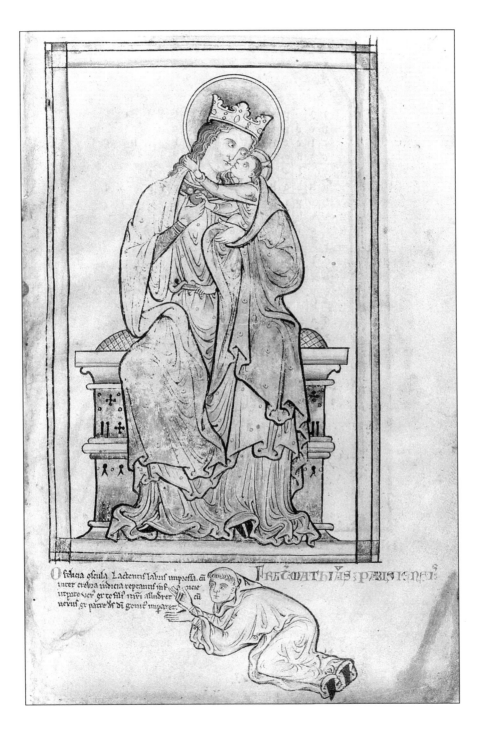

community. By the beginning of the thirteenth century, however, there is increasing evidence of manuscripts being written and illuminated to the order of private individuals for their personal use and enjoyment. Most of the finest and most famous books of subsequent generations were clearly influenced to some extent by the taste and by the pocket of the patron who would eventually pay the bill.

Very few of the craftsmen who produced these beautiful pages have left any record of themselves. Even the patrons are largely unidentifiable, though personal evidence such as heraldry becomes more common in later books. It is very hard to dispel the ingrained popular belief that all illuminated manuscripts were made by monks, toiling away for the glory of God in draughty Gothic cloisters. The scene was recently brought vividly to life in the film of *The Name of the Rose*, during which the cameras roamed around a vast and dimly lit scriptorium, where an assortment of unsavoury-looking fourteenth-century brethren was enthusiastically at work. Their output embraced books of very varied types and periods. In fact, by the beginning of the thirteenth century, much of the luxury end of the book trade seems already to have been in the hands of professionals, who often lived grouped together in particular areas of such centres as Paris or Oxford. It also appears that some of these people must have been prepared to move from place to place as work became available.

Paradoxically, however, one of the few named artists producing illustrated manuscripts in England during the early part of the thirteenth century was in fact a Benedictine monk, Matthew Paris of St Albans. Matthew was born about 1200 and died in 1259. Although he spent most of his life in a monastic community, he was by no means cut off from the world, for St Albans was a popular staging post and entertained the leading personalities of the day from both Church and State. It is implied in his writings that he was personally present on several historic occasions, including the translation of the relics of St Thomas Becket at Canterbury in 1220 and the marriage of Henry III to Eleanor of Provence in 1236. Matthew was basically a historian and his chronicles constitute one of the most important surviving sources for his time. He had the instincts of a journalist and gleaned first-hand accounts of many of the events which he described from those who passed through the guest house of the abbey. He was also an accomplished artist, adding with his own hand the coloured drawings that embellish most of his original manuscripts. In his most celebrated image, the full-page picture of the Virgin and Child prefixed to his *Historia Anglorum* in the British Library, he included his own portrait, prostrate in prayer at the Virgin's feet.

Although his formal historical work is written in Latin prose, Matthew also composed several works in Anglo-Norman French verse. These are lives of four English saints: Alban, patron of his own abbey, Thomas Becket and Edmund Rich of Canterbury, and Edward the Confessor. The Alban manuscript, now in Dublin, was apparently both written and illustrated by Matthew himself. It includes some personal notes which suggest that this type of book was prepared for circulation among the great ladies of the court, for their private enjoyment. French would have been the appropriate language for the purpose. The life of Edmund survives only in a later, unillustrated copy. What is generally believed to be the Becket is now represented only by a fragment of four leaves, neither written nor illustrated by the author, but with eight lively drawings by another hand. These leaves were sold in London in 1986 for well over £1 million and have since been deposited on loan at the British Library by J. Paul Getty. A complete copy of the life of Edward the Confessor is however preserved in Cambridge University Library. Although neither script nor illustrations can be attributed to Matthew Paris himself, the style and format of the book is very similar to that of the life of St Alban.

Edward was specially revered as the second founder of Westminster Abbey, adopted by the kings of England as their ceremonial church. In Matthew's day, Henry III was about to embark upon the major rebuilding programme which left the church much as we see it today, and in 1262 he translated Edward to a new shrine in the sanctuary. The drawing reproduced on page 80 purports to show the original burial of the saint some 200 years earlier, in 1066, although the officiating clergy are vested in the style of the thirteenth rather than the eleventh century. The 'portholes' in the base of the tomb allowed disabled pilgrims to approach as closely as possible to the virtue of the saint's relics.

Matthew Paris's illustrated saints' lives were not the only picture books available to his aristocratic public. The Book of Revelation, the Apocalypse of St John, enjoyed a tremendous vogue in England from the mid-thirteenth century and attracted a complex pictorial cycle, often carried out in coloured line drawing similar to that favoured by Matthew. On this account, a number of the Apocalypse manuscripts have been associated with the scriptorium of St Albans, although there is little direct evidence to support such a claim. The finest of these manuscripts, now in the library of Trinity College, Cambridge, is however fully illuminated in gold and colours. It is possibly the earliest of the English-made apocalypses and is usually dated slightly before the middle of the thirteenth century. Like the saints' lives, it has a French text and there is every appearance that it was designed for

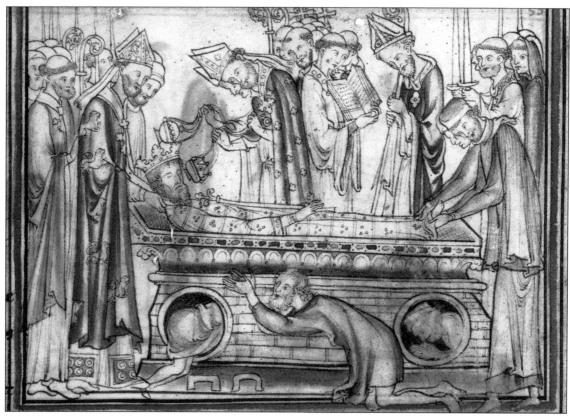

The burial of Edward the Confessor – another of Matthew Paris's 'Lives'. Though not from the artist's hand, it is similar to his personally illustrated 'Life of St Alban'.

personal use. So extravagantly decorated a book must have been commissioned for a very wealthy patron and it is not impossible that it was meant for Queen Eleanor, though there is no clear evidence of her ownership. In its illustrations, the contemporary rubs shoulders with the fabulous. The dragon and its evil allies are thrust into the mouth of hell by an angel, while the last battle rages between forces protected by weapons and chain mail suitable for warriors of the Seventh Crusade or the Barons' War.

Because Matthew Paris's name is known and his style can be identified with certainty, his manuscripts have attracted perhaps rather more attention than they merit. They are frequently used as a focus for other work of the period. It is very rare for the name of a medieval illuminator to be recorded, but there is a second English example almost exactly contemporary with the monk from St Albans, namely W. de Brailes. The latter appended his name several times to miniatures in the expensive, but not particularly inspired, illuminated manuscripts which he produced about 1230–60. He was probably the William de Brailes who is recorded as living in Cat Street in Oxford, on the site now occupied by the chapel of All Souls College. His greatest distinction lies in having been responsible for what appears to be the earliest independent book of hours of English origin.

The book of hours has with justification been described as the biggest best-seller of the Middle Ages. Between the middle of the thirteenth century and the Reformation, thousands upon thousands of copies were produced throughout Europe to suit all tastes and every pocket. However, in England this particular form of personal devotion did not achieve the instant popularity that it enjoyed on the other side of the Channel. Only some two dozen examples represent the period before 1350 and none of these ranks with the major masterpieces of the time, though each is a very individual little book, betraying clearly the taste and influence of its patron. The choice of illustrations is often both idiosyncratic and of immediate contemporary interest. One early fourteenth-century book of hours in the Bodleian Library in Oxford includes a miniature in which England's patron, St George, is paired with Thomas of Lancaster, cousin of Edward II, who was beheaded as a traitor in 1322 and thereafter regarded in some partisan circles as a martyr.

The type of devotional book most likely to be sumptuously and expensively illuminated for personal devotional use in England was the psalter, firmly established in fashion from the late twelfth century. Many of the early examples include major cycles of scenes from the life of Christ. Illustrated calendars, essential to the proper celebration of the feasts of the Church year, and richly painted initials, often devoted to scenes from the story of David, are also extant. A particularly splendid mid-thirteenth-century example is the Rutland Psalter, so named because it was owned by the dukes of Rutland prior to its acquisition by the British Library in 1983. Among its illustrations is a magnificent miniature of King David as a musician, pounding away on the keyboard of an organ as the notes which he is producing float above him in the guise of angels' heads. We do not know for whom this handsome book was originally intended. It has, however, a special place in the history of the English illuminated manuscript because it is the first book of its kind to incorporate scenes from contemporary life into the marginal decoration of some of its pages. Such scenes were to become a particular characteristic of the work of the early fourteenth century and are especially prominent in some of the outstanding psalters associated with people and places in East Anglia.

For sheer volume of pictorial content, Queen Mary's Psalter, one of the greatest treasures of the British Library, has few serious rivals. This superb book, made about 1310–20, opens with 118 pages of coloured line drawings of scenes from the Old Testament, from the Creation to the death of Solomon, each accompanied by an explanatory caption in French. After three pages of miniatures devoted to the ancestors and family of Christ and to the prophets and apostles, it offers a calendar with full-scale miniatures, both of the labours of the months and of the signs of the zodiac. The main Latin text is punctuated by fifty-four miniatures and nine historiated initials, of subjects from the life of Christ, followed by scenes from the lives of saints. In addition, the body of the book, from the second page of the psalms to the end of the text, is embellished in the lower margins with 464 delicately tinted drawings which embrace subjects from the bestiary, scenes from everyday courtly life such as hunting or tilting, sequences from popular religious mythology such as the apocryphal miracles of the Virgin, lives and passions of saints, and a selection of the fanciful beasts and monsters familiar in most of the decorated manuscripts of the period.

This manuscript thus offered its original owner not just a luxury book of devotion but an entire library of courtly picture books, both religious and secular, with subject matter to suit every mood. So lavish in concept is it that commentators have often been tempted to insist that it can only have been intended for a member of the royal family, possibly even a king. Nevertheless, against this attractive notion it must be remembered that illuminated books demonstrably made for English kings, queens and princes during the thirteenth and fourteenth centuries are few and seldom approach the stature of this superb book. It seems astonishing by modern standards that so supreme a work of art, probably costing quite literally a king's (or at least a nobleman's) ransom, should offer no clue at all to its origins. Indeed, as early as 1553 its beauty so struck the sensibilities of a customs officer that he refused to permit it to leave the country, presenting it instead to Queen Mary Tudor, whose name it now bears.

The artist of Queen Mary's Psalter presented a more than somewhat idealized portrait of the society of his day. The activities of its marginal sequences are definitely those of the leisured classes. Even the farming scenes in the calendar seem to lack any element of urgency or honest sweat. This is not so in another famous early fourteenth-century manuscript, the Luttrell Psalter, also now in the British Library but originally commissioned by a Lincolnshire landowner, Sir Geoffrey Luttrell, probably about 1325–35. Ever since it became widely known at the end of the nineteenth century, this book has provided publishers with a major source for pictures of rural life in England 500 years ago.

We know quite a lot about Sir Geoffrey and his family from the local records of the time, and they are still commemorated in the church at Irnham, the small Lincolnshire village where they lived. The only large miniature in the psalter is dedicated to Sir Geoffrey himself, who is seen with his wife and daughter-in-law (a daughter of Geoffrey le Scrope, chief justice of the King's Bench), all decked out in heraldic garments that leave no doubt at all about the ownership of the book. Apart from conventional historiated initials at the divisions of the psalter, the decoration of this manuscript is confined to its margins and presents, alongside a magnificent array of monsters and grotesques and a selection of figures of saints, a full and unidealized picture of everyday life and work in the Luttrell village. That this life was no easy one is not concealed from the spectator. The physical effort involved in weeding or clod breaking, in pushing a heavily laden harvest wagon uphill, in lugging one's grain to the mill, and even in chopping up meat for the lord's table, is clear to the eye. However, relaxation and entertainment are not forgotten. There is a splendid bear-baiting group and many pictures of contemporary games, some now hard to identify. The somewhat coarse style of the main Luttrell illuminator, very far removed from the almost cloying sweetness of some of the drawings of the Queen Mary artist, adds to the general sense of verisimilitude. He creates a distinct impression of having truly observed the world he was setting down on his pages and many of his more memorable characters, including the little curly-tailed dog seen sitting menacingly outside the windmill and, on another page, barking rapturously in pursuit of predatory birds, are surely drawn from life.

Akin to the Luttrell Psalter in artistic approach, though not in content and purpose, is the Holkham Bible Picture Book, which may also have been painted soon after 1325. This manuscript entered the British Library collection from that of the earls of Leicester, whose seat is Holkham Hall, not so very far away from Irnham. The original provenance of the volume is, however, unknown. It is a very unusual book, containing some 230 scenes, largely from the Old and New Testaments, which could have been used as a visual aid to popular religious teaching. The figure of a Dominican friar appears at the beginning of the manuscript, bearing a scroll which exhorts the artist to do his work well as it is intended for the eyes of the rich. He may have been the originator of the scheme of illustration and also author of the brief commentaries explaining the various scenes which are written, like those of the Queen Mary Psalter biblical pictures, in French.

When these pictures are projected on to a blank surface, they readily assume the appearance of wall paintings. They are on a larger scale than most manuscript illustrations and the technique is closer to coloured drawing than to painting. In some cases, the backgrounds are filled with patterns which emulate fabrics, elsewhere the vellum is left uncoloured. The features of the characters are so boldly drawn as to suggest caricature or theatrical make-up. Indeed, the exaggerated poses of many of the figures and the inclusion of numerous popular apocryphal episodes, such as the

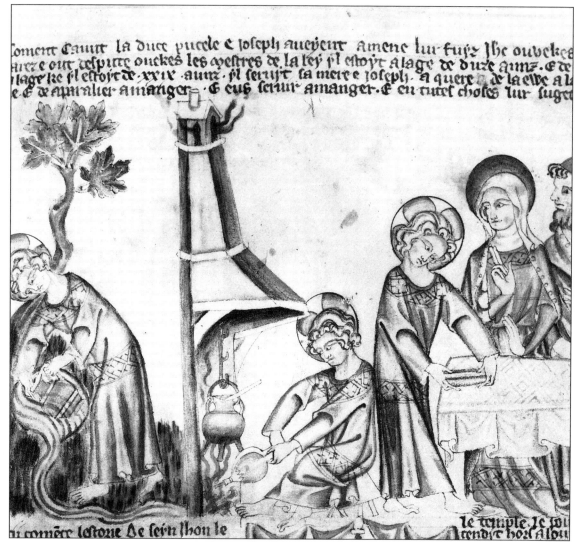

The Christ Child at work in the house of his parents, from the Holkham Bible Picture Book (c. 1325), incorporating a scene of medieval cooking skills.

story of the blacksmith's wicked wife, who forged the nails for the Crucifixion (which was recently seized upon by an advocate of female equality, who innocently supposed it to be a simple picture of a medieval woman at work in a man's world), do strongly suggest the influence of contemporary religious drama. Like the Luttrell Psalter, this book has a good deal to offer in the way of pictures of everyday life, though here applied to biblical situations such as the agricultural activities of Cain and Abel and of the shepherds at Bethlehem, or the household chores undertaken by the Christ Child in the home of his earthly parents. His cooking fire is provided with a very workmanlike chimney, designed to counteract the effects of a down-draught.

The end of the fourteenth century saw a return to fashion of richly decorated, large-scale service books for use in public worship. Several of these were made for the churches of major religious communities. Although their avowed purpose was to glorify God and to ensure the welfare of the souls of their patrons, these books do tend to be employed in addition as vehicles for the advertisement of the wealth and status, both of the patrons and of the community involved. One splendid example, weighing approximately three stone, was made about 1400 for the Benedictine abbey of Sherborne in Dorset. For generations, it has belonged to the dukes of Northumberland and is at present on loan to the British Library. This manuscript seems to have been a joint commission by the Bishop of Salisbury, Richard Mitford, and the Abbot of Sherborne, Robert Bruyning. The figure of the abbot may be recognized at least a hundred times among the marginal decorations of the book. The bishop is seen on eight occasions, perhaps reflecting the modest proportion of his contribution. Both the craftsmen mainly responsible for the work — the Benedictine scribe John Whas and the Dominican illuminator John Siferwas — are depicted in half a dozen places. The missal also contains a most complicated programme of subjects devoted to the status and possessions of the monastery of Sherborne.

Some fifteen years earlier, Abbot Nicholas Litlyngton of Westminster determined that his abbey church should be provided with a new and splendid missal. As head of the monastic community serving England's royal ceremonial church, he was able to provide in his new service book the prayer forms required for use at coronations and royal funerals, as well as the normal cycle of masses for the ecclesiastical year. Like the Abbot of Sherborne, he had his connection with the manuscript underlined on many of its pages, his arms and monogram appearing frequently in the decoration. Furthermore, he had his arms painted on the outside edges, so that he would even be remembered when the book was lying closed. Litlyngton's Missal is still among the treasures of Westminster Abbey and, by great good fortune, so too is the account roll for 1383–4 on which the payments for its production are recorded. From this we learn that its scribe, Thomas Preston, was a professional, housed and clothed at the expense of the abbot for the two years during which he worked on the commission. The vellum cost £4. 6s. 8d., the embroidery of the covers 6s. 8d. and the illumination £23. 0s. 3d., with an extra 10s. for the very splendid Crucifixion miniature

plane legendo et non dicatur
Dominus vobiscum neque Oremus.
set tm V Adiutorium nostrum in nomine domini.

Exorciso te
creatura
salis per de-
um uiu-
um. per
deum
uerum. per
deum sanctum et per deum qui te per Eli-
seum prophetam in aquam mitti
iussit ut sanaretur sterilitas a-
que: ut efficiaris sal exorcizatus
in salutem credencium. et sis omnibus te sumentibus sanitas anime et
corporis. et effugiat atque discedat
ab eo loco quo aspersus fueris
omnis fantasia nequicie uel
uersucia diabolice fraudis. omni-
sque spiritus immundus adiuratus
per eum qui uenturus est iudicare uiuos et mortuos et seculum per
ignem. Oracio

Immensam clemenciam tuam
omnipotens eterne deus humi-
liter imploramus: ut hanc cre-
aturam salis quam in usum
humani generis tribuisti bene-
dicere et sanctificare tua pi-
etate digneris: ut sit omnibus

sumentibus salus mentis et corporis. et quicquid eo tactum uel
respersum fuerit careat omni in-
mundicia. omnique impugna-
cione spiritalis nequicie. Per uirtutem eiusdem domini nostri ihesu
qui uenturus est iudicare uiuos
et mortuos et seculum per ignem.

Exorcismus aque

Exorciso te creatura aque
in nomine dei patris
omnipotentis. et in nomine ihesu
cristi filii eius domini nostri et
in uirtute spiritus sancti: ut fias a-
qua exorcizata ad effugandam
omnem potestatem inimici. et ip-
sum inimicum eradicare et ex-
plantare ualeas cum angelis
suis apostaticis. per uirtutem eiusdem domini nostri ihesu cristi qui uen-

Deus qui ad salutem
humani generis maxi-
ma queque sacramenta in aqua-
rum substancia condidisti. ad-
esto inuocacionibus nostris et ele-
mento huic multimodis pu-
rificacionibus preparato uirtutem
tue benedictionis infunde
ut creatura tua misteriis tuis
seruiens. ad abiciendos demo-
nes morbosque pellendos diui-
ne gracie sumat effectum: ut

that precedes the Canon of the Mass. Unfortunately the illuminators are not named. Some idea of the comparative cost of the enterprise may be gained from the fact that the overall expenditure of £34. 14s. 7d. assigned to the missal represents approximately a tenth of the total sum paid out by the abbot's treasurer during the period covered by the account roll.

The books mentioned thus far are divided between two languages, Latin for the more formal texts and French for popular use. At the end of the fourteenth century, a literature in the English language itself came rapidly to prominence. In this respect England was following a pattern already established elsewhere in Europe, particularly in Italy. Its authors were not infrequently cultured men in public life who had enjoyed, either personally or vicariously, the benefits of travel abroad and had thus come into contact with the work of such modern authors as Dante and Boccaccio.

The supreme example of this new vernacular literature is Chaucer's *Canterbury Tales*, which seems to have taken shape about 1386–9 when the author, temporarily out of favour at court (where he had already enjoyed thirty years of royal service), was living in retirement in Kent, in close proximity to the Canterbury road. Chaucer's tales, in their narrative framework, achieved an instant popularity. His party of pilgrims from all walks of society — from the dandified Squire to the unsavoury Summoner, and from the fastidious Prioress to the pleasure-loving Wife of Bath — clearly rang true with their contemporary audience. Today they provide the social historian with a lively source of human information with which to flesh out more sober sources for the pilgrimage to Becket's shrine. These were the folk whose devotions were lit by the candles so meticulously enumerated in the 1428 customary of the shrine, and who were refreshed by its guardians with bread, cheese and beer if their exertions proved too much for them. More than eighty manuscript copies of Chaucer's most famous book can still be identified; it was first printed by Caxton in 1478, and it has remained in print and in favour ever since.

But, surprisingly enough, the literary endeavours of Chaucer and his contemporaries did not provide English illuminators with a wide new field in which to exercise their imaginations. Although vernacular books, both translations and original works, were in other countries accompanied by appropriate cycles of illustration, decorated literary manuscripts in England very seldom boast any pictures. An Italian work such as Dante's *Divine Comedy* might attract a miniature cycle as rich as that found in a thirteenth-century English apocalypse, but the *Canterbury Tales* remain unillustrated. The famous figures of the pilgrims from the Ellesmere Chaucer, now in the Huntington Library in California, are virtually unique

A page from the Litlyngton Missal, used for all the services of the ecclesiastical year as well as for special royal ceremonies. Its commissioning by the Abbot of Westminster in the 1380s illustrates the fashion of richly decorated, large-scale books for use in public.

and set no pattern for the future. However, the features of Chaucer himself were enshrined for us through the good offices of one of his fellow writers, Thomas Hoccleve. Hoccleve was Clerk of the Privy Seal and a professional scribe. He was also a fervent admirer of Chaucer and strove to emulate his work. In a copy of his own *Regimen of Princes*, in the British Library, he caused to be painted a portrait of his hero in accordance with his own memories of his features, 'to putte othir men in remembraunce of his persone'. All subsequent pictures of the poet are apparently descended from this image.

Illuminated manuscripts of all kinds can thus supply us with intimate views of the past, often preserving the very personal interests and outlook of the men and women who invested in them for pleasure, for status, for learning, for the good of their souls or for the glory of God. The artists and patrons of thirteenth- and fourteenth-century England have immeasurably enriched our knowledge of their times and their largely anonymous masterpieces continue to delight, to awe, and sometimes even to amuse us.

The father of English literature? A portrait of Geoffrey Chaucer enshrined by his fellow-writer and admirer, Thomas Hoccleve, in his early fifteenth-century Regimen of Princes.

How he þt haunt was mayden marie
Ans lat his loue floure and fructifie

Al þogh his lyfe be queynt þe resemblaunce
Of hym hap in me so fressh lyflynesse
Þat to putte othir men in remembraunce
Of his persone I haue heere his lyknesse
Do make to þis ende in soothfastnesse
Þat þei þt haue of hym lest þought & mynde
By þis peynture may ageyn hym fynde

The ymages þt in þe chirche been
Maken folk þenke on god & on his seyntes
Whan þe ymages þei beholden & seen
Were oft vnsyte of hem causith restreyntes
Of þoughtes gode Whan a þing depeynt is
Or entayled if men take of it heede
Thoght of þe lyknesse it wil in hym brede

Yit some holden oppynyon and sey
Þat none ymages schuld I maked be
Þei erren foule & goon out of þe wey
Of trouth haue þei scant sensibilite
Passe ou þt now blessid trinite
Vpon my maistres soule mercy haue
ffor hym lady eke þt I mercy craue

VII MEDIEVAL KINGSHIP
Arthur in English Romance

Brian Stone

Quotations are from Sir Thomas Malory, *Le Morte Darthur* (Everyman, 1906, reprinted 1978), which will be referred to as Malory; and the two poems, the stanzaic *Le Morte Arthur*, referred to as *SMA*, and the alliterative *Morte Arthure*, referred to as *AMA*. Both poems are quoted in the modern verse translations by Brian Stone. *King Arthur's Death: Morte Arthure and Le Morte Arthur* (Penguin, 1988). The translation of *SMA* is free, and in ballad style.

'THOUGH YE BE OUR KING in that degree, ye are but a knight as we are, and ye are sworn unto knighthood as well as we.' Thus Sir Mador (Malory) to King Arthur. The circumstance was that Mador's cousin Sir Patrise had been poisoned by an apple handed to him in innocence by Queen Guinevere, but intended by the poisoner for Sir Gawain; and Mador, requiring justice from Arthur, found it slow in coming. Significantly, in the French source, *La Mort le Roi Artu*, Arthur at first entertains the idea that Guinevere may be guilty, but neither Malory nor the poet of the *SMA*, both Englishmen, so tarnish the image of England's mythical hero-king. As a super-knight among knights, but nevertheless himself 'but a knight', he should appear doubly just: he should not only set in motion the formal processes of the law, but also be motivated by an inward feeling for natural justice.

Malory generally insists on Arthur's perfection as a chivalric justicer and, like a good medieval preacher, he also gives prominence to exemplars of Arthur's opposite, like King Mark of the Tristram episodes. On one occasion, disguised in black, Mark attacks two of his guests from Arthur's court who are out on a night ride, and is beaten. His adversary, Sir Gaheris, having found out who he is, answers his plea for mercy with: 'Thou art a king anointed with chrism, and therefore thou shouldest hold with all men

Kingly virtue: Arthur. Late fourteenth-century tapestry by Nicholas Bataille.

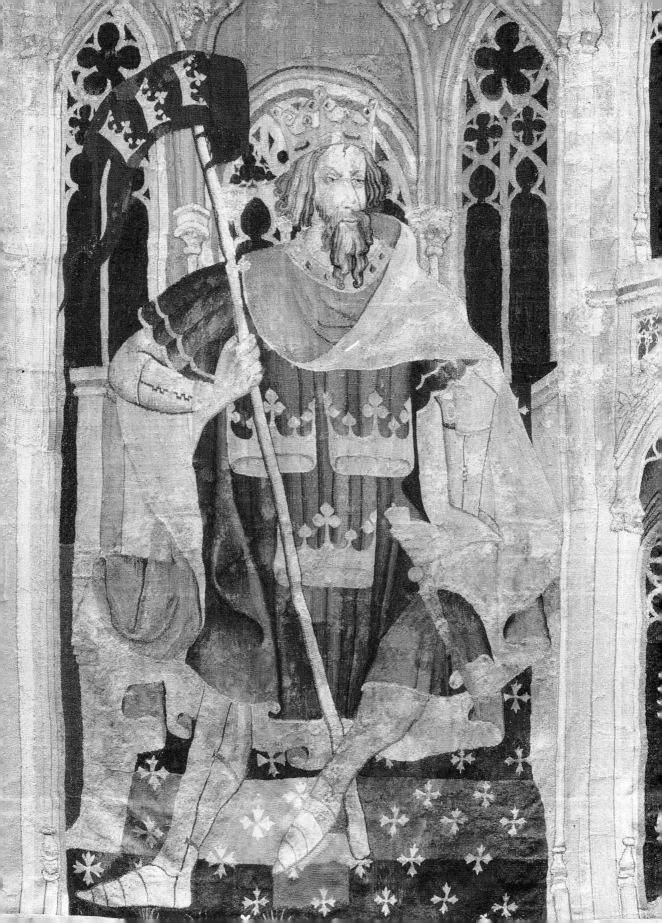

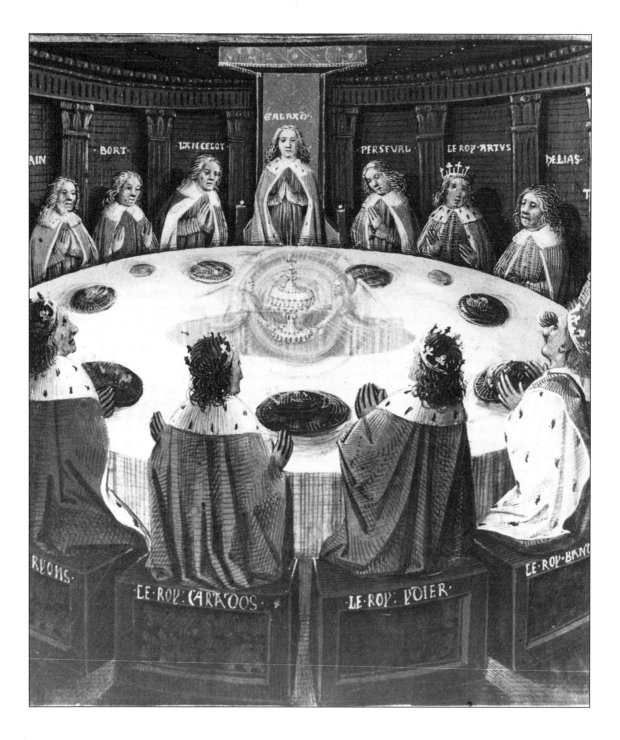

of worship; and therefore thou art worthy to die' (Malory). As Lamorak says to Tristram, in contrasting Mark and Arthur, 'The honour of both courts be not alike.'

The anointing with chrism and the obligation to hold with all men of worship were the two cornerstones of the ideal of kingship in both the literature and the society of the time. Each carried a wealth of conceptions and assumptions, not all of which sort well together, though most of them bear on each other. The moral and spiritual obligations of accepting chrism on the one hand, and the attaining and holding of worship (=honour) on the other, were bound to be in frequent conflict. Such essential qualifications for knighthood as noble blood, wealth and murderous courage in conflict — to leave aside for the moment Christian devotion, loyalty and generosity, and the obligations to be humble, courteous and kind to women — are against the spirit of the Beatitudes. The two special knightly qualities of prowess, which means courage and all the skills of fighting including leadership, and of largesse, which means spiritual as well as practical generosity, underpin all other qualities, because prowess derives from rank and conquest, and the exercise of largesse depends on the ability to give. What was true of knights was even more true of kings.

Edward III, who set up the Order of the Garter in 1348, was the second of the many medieval European kings and princes to found a secular order of knighthood. Like his formidable warrior grandfather, Edward I, he was an Arthurian enthusiast, who took King Arthur and his Round Table as patterns of chivalry. Not surprisingly, Maurice Keen writes: 'Fifteenth-century chivalric literature is a little more true to life than is sometimes recognized.'

Edward III died in 1377, and the other warrior king of England of the period was Henry V (1413–22); a reading public of their or immediately subsequent times would expect some verisimilitude in the literary treatment of matters they knew about in real life, such as government, wars and jousting.

The three literary works upon which I shall mainly draw in discussing kingship are the stanzaic *Le Morte Arthur* (*c.* 1350), the alliterative *Morte Arthure* (*c.* 1400), and Malory's prose epic *Le Morte Darthur* (*c.* 1470, printed 1485 by Caxton). All are infused with English fourteenth- and fifteenth-century ideas and detail, and the *AMA* in particular is full of topical reference, while the magical and folkloristic matter of the twelfth- and thirteenth-century sources — Geoffrey of Monmouth, Wace, Layamon and so on — is severely curtailed. King Arthur's fight with the Giant of Mont St Michel, and Sir Gawain's fight against Sir Priamus, whose sword caused

A vision of the Holy Grail appears on the Round Table to King Arthur and his knights. From a fourteenth-century French manuscript, Le Roman de Lancelot du Lac.

unstaunchable wounds wherever it struck, are the only important magical episodes in the *AMA* which occur to me. Both are also treated by Malory, who bases his accounts mainly on the alliterative poem. I do not refer to the best of the English Arthurian romances, *Sir Gawain and the Green Knight*, because in it the role of Arthur, as the holder of the chivalric ring within which Gawain tackles his moral and religious problem, is largely formal.

As the nonpareil in armed combat, the remote national king from whose pseudo-history Edward I and Edward III sought to derive their ritual strength as heroic monarchs was an equivocal figure. In French Arthurian literature, he appears often weak and indecisive, as if he were turning a blind eye to his queen's adultery with Lancelot, perhaps because he sets uniquely high value on the chivalric support he receives from the adulterer — an outstanding example of the way in which the literature of male-orientated societies, from earliest times until at least the eighteenth century, sets honour between man and man above honour between man and woman. In actual combat, whether in war or tourney, this king tends to be closely supported by knights, whose help he requires after defeating two or three adversaries. But in some of the earliest versions and in several English romances, he is a warrior excelled not even by Lancelot, who can kill twenty — the standard number — or more of the enemy in a single sally. 'And Arthur was so bloody, that by his shield there might no man know him, for all was blood and brains on his sword' (Malory). In this kind of manifestation, Arthur sometimes exhibits the kind of grim humour which is found in Icelandic saga and Anglo-Saxon epic. In the great battle against the Roman Empire which forms the centre-piece of the *AMA*, Arthur

> Got close to Golopas, who had done greatest harm,
> And cut him in two clean through the knees.
> 'Come down!' said the King, 'And account for it to your fellows!
> You are too high by half, I have to tell you.
> You'll be even handsomer soon, with Our Lord's help!'
> And with his steely sword he struck off his head.
>
> *(AMA)*

A fourteenth-century round table, now in the Great Hall at Winchester. It was decorated by Henry VII with his own Tudor rose, and he named his son, born in 1486, Arthur.

As a general, Arthur often holds his own force in reserve while he watches those of his loyal knights or allies conduct the opening exchanges. At the siege of Metz, though he reconnoitres the position personally, exposing himself carelessly to shots from the walls, Arthur notes that his French allies are fighting so feebly that he has to send a foraging force to find meat for them to eat, and he takes no part in the routing of the Duke of Lorraine's army outside the walls, before conducting the siege himself. The same

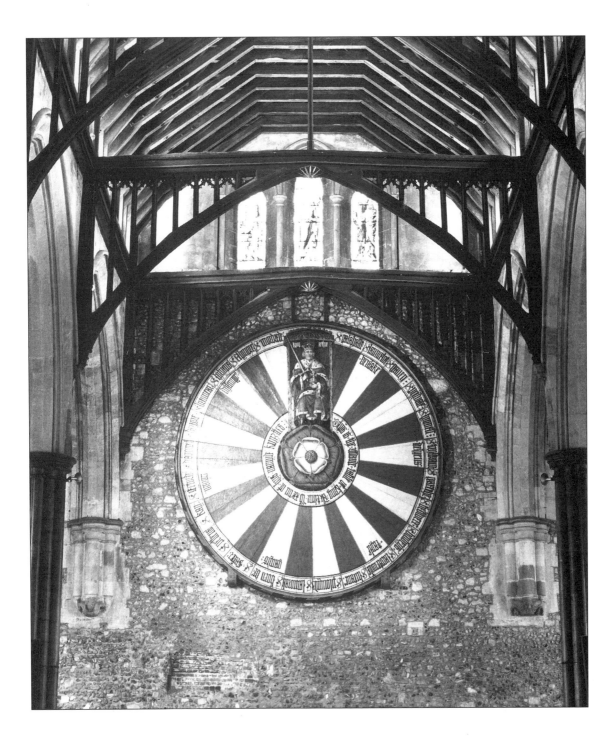

principle of holding his own force in reserve, in order to complete a victory, was followed at Crécy, where Edward III divided his army in three, and led the reserve third himself.

At Crécy the chivalrous spirit of the French knights led them to disaster: approaching the English position with the evening sun in their faces, they decided to attack at once instead of waiting to attack the following morning with the rising sun behind them, as they had been advised. In comparable chivalric spirit, the blind King of Bohemia rode with them, and was killed. In the *AMA*, Arthur shows the same kind of tactical sense as Edward; when not prepared for a particular attack from the Romans

> . . .our wily King was wary and watched for this force,
> And wisely withdrew his warriors from the woods,
> But had the fires fed so that they flamed up high
> As they trussed up their trappings and stole away.
>
> *(AMA)*

Another resort of England's ideal king in this poem is the *chevauchée*, the medieval equivalent of scorching the earth. As the word indicates, a *chevauchée* is a mounted raid. The king refrains from this raping, looting and burning while fighting in the French territories that he regards as his own, but uses it from Lorraine to Italy, being particularly severe on Tuscany. Lucius conducts a *chevauchée* through France, on his way to do battle with Arthur, and in the *SMA* Arthur conducts one in Lancelot's French dominions when prosecuting both Gawain's feud with Lancelot and his own revenge for the famous adultery. The *chevauchée* was a frequent resort of Edward's armies in France: his sweep from the Cotentin peninsula to Calais, fighting Crécy on the way, is well known, and the Black Prince similarly ravaged the vineyard region in the south-west during the campaign the main battle of which was at Poitiers (1346). There John II of France was captured, after which he languished as a prisoner in England until his ransom was paid. But then the hostages who replaced him escaped, and he felt in honour bound to return to London, where he died in 1364.

That was the kind of punctilio Arthur generally observes in medieval romance. He is scrupulous about ransom, but usually tries to rescue those of his knights who have been captured, before the battle ends. On the other hand, when the situation is particularly difficult, or the enemy has behaved atrociously, as Mordred did before and during the last battle, then Arthur orders that no quarter be given. However, when he takes an enemy city, such as Metz or Como, he responds to pleas from noble female citizens, and forbids his men to rape or kill them, or to attack or despoil children or holy men and women. It seems that Edward tried without success to prevent his men looting and raping in Caen during his Crécy campaign, and with some reluctance responded to the pleas of the burghers of Calais. To show mercy after a successful siege was to blunt a main aim of medieval warfare: the acquisition of loot.

Other ideals reflecting actual practice may be noted in the fictional Arthur's battle repertoire. He displays his own true banner and shield, unlike Mordred, who 'Because of his cowardice cast off his own device' *(AMA)*. In contrast, Arthur exhorts his men:

> Neither attend nor protect me, nor take account of me,
> But be busy about my banners with your bright weapons,
> Ensuring that strong knights sternly defend them,
> And hold them nobly high for our army to see.
>
> *(AMA)*

Arthur's battlefield orations, vows and encomiums over the dead in this poem *(AMA)* are perhaps the best expression of heroic medieval spirit to be found anywhere, and they constantly remind the reader of their Anglo-Saxon precursors in *Beowulf* and the *Anglo-Saxon Chronicle*. The description of the king's grief over the dead Gawain, his expressions of lamentation and his vow to avenge his cousin make that passage one of the most moving in medieval literature. And his speeches in the face of his own imminent death after killing Mordred, unlike those containing the mystical concerns of the dying Arthur in the *SMA* and Malory, which are memorably caught by Tennyson, express the fundamental responsibilities of royal leadership: recognition of mutual service between king and lieger, recognition of achievement, provision for the succession and for his own burial, forgiveness to Guinevere, thanks to God and a final *'In manus'*. Here are the first six lines:

> 'O King rightly crowned, in care I am left!
> All my lordship is laid low to the ground.
> Those who gave me gifts through the grace of God,
> Maintained my majesty by their might in battle,
> And set me up in honour as Earth's master,
> In a terrible time this trouble has come to them . . .'
>
> *(AMA)*

This matter of speech, whether it is made by or to the model of kingship, is important because through it the relation between king and subject is made

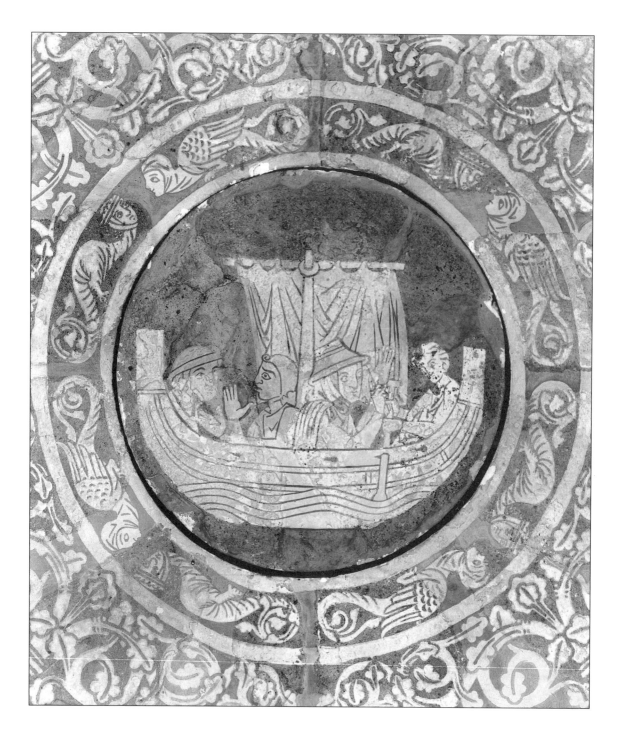

explicit, in both meaning and tone, on the chief issues which affect them jointly: such issues as government policy, allegiance, alliances, personal and social justice, promotions and rewards, dynastic arrangements. The orations are found in all the Arthurian works so far mentioned, but are almost always more detailed, and more in accordance with the ideal practice in the real world, in the *AMA*. After a generous courtly feast, policy is decided in council, with the king opening the subject (such as replying to the demand that Arthur pay tribute and yield sovereignty to Rome). Members of the assembly speak in turn, in order of rank. On the occasion cited, the heir to the throne, Cador, speaks first, followed by the kings of Scotland, Brittany and Wales. When Lancelot's turn comes, he stresses that he is one of the 'lesser men'. Each of the six speakers recommends war on Rome, and all except Cador specify the number and kind of troops they will contribute to the campaign, and vow to perform a particular deed of prowess or revenge for past indignities. Though most vows in the romances call on divine personages, here each subject of Arthur's swears by Saint Veronica, patron saint of pilgrimage, which is ironically appropriate for soldiers who have Rome as their campaign target. On other occasions, kings and knights may swear by their own names, or by their lands, as King Mark does (Malory).

Each of the vowed feats is achieved during the subsequent battles against Rome, hundreds of lines later, which shows that the making and fulfilling of vows in the presence of royalty is structural in this kind of literature. A similar debate, though without the detail, appears in the *SMA*, the true hero of which is Lancelot, when he is exercising his kingship in his French province of Benwick (Bayonne? or in Brittany?). The subject there is whether Lancelot should continue his passive resistance to the forces of Arthur and Gawain which are laying waste his lands, or issue from his stronghold and defeat them. When Lancelot eventually battles against the king who originally knighted him, his response to the unhorsing of Arthur in the ensuing conflict is chivalrous in the highest imaginable degree:

> 'Alas,' said Lancelot, 'What woe
>   That ever I should see
> Unhorsed before my very eyes
>   The King who knighted me!'
> And then, dismounting from his steed
>   — So generous was he! —
> He horsed the King on it, telling him
>   Out of harm's way to flee.
>
>   (*SMA*)

Tristan with Isolde, King Mark's betrothed, crossing to Cornwall accompanied by Isolde's waiting woman, Brangane. A thirteenth-century floor tile from Chertsey Abbey.

One further element in the speech-making and council-holding processes must be mentioned. When faced with the enemy, the ideal king does not commit his forces to battle before offering a final parley, in order to establish the justice of his cause and to confirm the inveterate hostility of his foe.

Most battles, and some individual tourneys, begin and end with religious grace notes. The vow of the resolve, with allowance for the will of God, begins the context, and, when the dust settles, God is given the credit. When the people of Brittany praise Arthur for killing the Giant of Mont St Michel, who raped their duchess and slit her to the navel in killing her, Arthur gives the credit to God alone before organizing the distribution of treasure from the giant's lair, and goes even further in religious celebration of the event, by setting up a monastery 'In memory of that martyr in her mountain resting-place' *(AMA)*. Similarly, in Malory, after slaughtering 30,000 in the battle of the Humber, Arthur 'kneeled down and thanked God meekly', and founded the Abbey of La Beale Adventure on the spot.

Yet in the romances as in real life there is constant tension between the Christian advocacy of peace and the heroic warrior's insistence on the resort of war. Just as throughout Edward's campaigns in France papal nuncios were always trying to prevent battles, so in the *SMA* a papal messenger visits Arthur in Carlisle to stop the war he and Gawain are waging:

> He read the letter of the Pope
>   For everyone to hear:
> 'The King must agree with Lancelot
>   And take back Guinevere;
> Their peace must be a lasting one
>   Or else, through their despite,
> All England shall be interdicted
>   And fall in wretched plight.'
>   *(SMA)*

The wills of Arthur and Lancelot to accept this ruling are frustrated by Gawain, who is intent on avenging the deaths of his brothers during Lancelot's rescue of Guinevere from the bale-fire.

As can be seen, the bonds of piety formally seal every event and activity for the ideal king. A king was secularly installed, but ecclesiastically crowned. The difference between a coronation and a knightly dubbing was that a knight was dubbed by a king or a noble of prowess, not a priest, though the ceremony of initiation into knighthood included a night vigil in church and other rituals. Maurice Keen notes that occasions appropriate for dubbing were when court was being held, when a crusade was being launched, and before battle. In the *AMA*, Arthur's dubbings usually take place in connection with a battle: before it starts, or during a lull. The emphasis is on the effect on morale, because a newly dubbed knight fights harder in order to express his pride and allegiance. In Malory, whose general process of narrative is geared more to tourney and individual joust than to warfare by armies, dubbings may take place at any time, and the emphasis is on the maturation process and the enlarging of nobility that dubbing achieves.

While ostensibly conducting wars for the greater glory of the Christian religion and increasing the stock of knightly men devoted to upholding the Cross — the late form of Arthur's arms included two crosses *argent*, with a Virgin and Child *or* in each — the ideal king of romance fulfilled several religious functions. In Malory's version of the Priamus episode already referred to, King Arthur gives Gawain permission to have Priamus christened before the final attack on Metz. Arthur's piety in battle is demonstrated when he deals with the dead, giving friend and foe equal rites of sanctity and honour, and doing his best to see that their bodies are returned to their birthplaces. It is true that in returning the bodies of Lucius and his nobles to Rome, Arthur with grim humour presents the coffins as the tribute Rome demanded of him in the first place; but

> They laid out and oiled those honoured bodies,
> Lapping them in sixty layers of linen
> And enclosing them in lead lest they decompose . . .
> With their banners above and their badges below.
>
> *(AMA)*

Since Arthurian romance of our period was composed against the background of the Crusades, the idea of Jerusalem as a goal and an opportunity for killing or converting pagans is often shown to be in the mind of the ideal king and his knights. Hence special emphasis is given to the heathen identity of enemies in the main works cited here; in the *AMA* in particular, great play is made with the hordes of oriental pagans and warlocks recruited into the emperor's forces, and on Arthur's return to England to deal with his usurping cousin Mordred (in Malory, he is the incestuous son), England is depicted as overrun by Scandinavian and other Northern European heathens whom Mordred has rewarded with lands and titles.

That largesse of Mordred's was illegal because he gave away what was not his; but Arthur's largesse, as a prime quality of an anointed king, is everywhere stressed. What he gives is his own, and it is given as reward for meritorious service. A conspicuous reward is the one he confers on the herald who brings him news of Gawain's victory outside Metz:

'High-spirited herald,' said Arthur, 'by Christ
You have healed my heart, I would have you know:
A hundred-pound holding in Hampton I freely give you!'
(AMA)

In Malory, after the fall of Metz, Arthur 'made dukes and earls, and made every man rich'; conferring titles on the deserving, as well as enriching them, is supreme largesse. In the matter of lavish entertaining and carelessness in the distribution of cash favours, the Roman ambassador reports back to Rome of Arthur:

Speak of him as a spender who despises silver,
Gives gold no more regard than great boulders,
Rates wine as water that wells from the ground,
And worships no wealth in this world but glory.
(AMA)

That value of the ideal king may be understood in the light of May McKisack's judgement on Edward III. He

. . .may fairly be charged with vanity, ostentation, and extravagance, if it
is remembered that Edward's subjects called these things by different
names and thought them proper to a king.

Concerning the attitude of the ideal king to womankind, there is nothing in the *AMA* except Mordred's treason in stealing Guinevere and getting her with child, and the resultant damage to Arthur's state, together with his instant and swiftly prosecuted resolve to take revenge. Guinevere's acceptance of Mordred is treated simply as treason. But in the *SMA* and in Malory, Guinevere resists Mordred by a trick, feigning a wish to buy wedding clothes in London, and there shutting herself up in the Tower with a strong defence.

Throughout French and English medieval romance, queens are like other women, that is to say, chattels with few formal rights in the dynastic and power structures of men, though they exist there on pedestals. Volition they have, particularly to fall in love and seduce men; and it is mostly women who exercise magical arts. But the context is usually one of male business, such as the offence to knightly chastity of a man who breaks a vow or a loyalty by making love outside the rules. The special queenly characteristic is to plead for the oppressed, as the ladies of Metz do, and as Chaucer's Hippolyta does in *The Knight's Tale*.

A paramount duty of a knight, and of that super-knight, a king, was to honour and defend women. It may be noted that Edward III took his wife Philippa and the many ladies of her court on shipboard into the dangerous naval battle of Sluys (1340), where he humiliated the French and so freed England's south coast from sea-borne raids for many years. He assigned Philippa as guard 300 men-at-arms (dismounted knights) and 500 archers. I find no such solicitous provision for queens in Arthurian romances.

The allocation of women in marriage is usually conducted by men — prospective husbands and fathers-in-law — the brides-to-be being scarcely consulted. It is illuminating that when the Arthurian stories reached Scandinavia, women are often consulted, and there are conspicuous cases of knights refusing to pursue their proposals because the women turn them down, and of the fathers accepting their daughters' refusals. That does not happen in English literature until after Shakespeare, except untypically, or when such a powerful duke of comedy as Theseus in *A Midsummer Night's Dream* craftily thwarts a testy and possessive father.

The ideal king, at least in early sources which Malory used, may express royal virility outside marriage; that is the privilege, like the occasional act of tyranny, which popular imagination accords a national hero. Arthur lusts for 'Lionors, a passing fair damosel', and 'had ado with her, and gat on her a child', and he fatally begets Mordred on Margawse, the wife of the Orkney king, Lot. At the time, Arthur does not know she is his half-sister, being the daughter of his mother Igraine and her husband the Duke of Cornwall. He is just lusting after a mother of four who happens to be visiting his court. But both those episodes took place before Arthur married Guinevere, and in their marriage it is she, through her long adulterous connection with Lancelot, who breaks the rule of chastity in royal marriage. In so doing, she poses the king the problem, when she is caught *in flagrante delicto*, of whether she should be burnt, the standard sentence for that kind of treason. Arthur does not waver in either Malory or the *SMA*, though it grieves him to follow his own laws in the case. But of course Lancelot, in rescuing Guinevere from the bale-fire, saves the king from the consequences of his altruistic behaviour. Even so, it should be emphasized that Arthur seems to express not jealousy, but only hurt, at the treason of his wife and best knight. The poet of the *SMA* annotates the moment briefly, but with due regard for the proprieties of justice, which include consultation between the king and his knights:

It was no time to take their ease:
　　Arthur in anguish drew
His knights to him in conference
　　To deem what they must do.
They all were keen to doom the Queen
　　The fate that she had earned;
That very day, without delay,
　　They said she must be burned.

(SMA)

Malory's judgement on Guinevere is contained in the extraordinary short chapter entitled 'How true love is likened to summer', which concludes Book XVIII: ' . . . while she lived she was a true lover, and therefore she had a good end'. Her guilt and penitence, and her acknowledgement that her sin brought ruin to the Round Table, are wonderfully expressed in the stanzaic poem.

It remains to consider briefly the factors of the imaginary which in all ages tend to collect round the idealized figure of majesty. In Arthurian romance they tend to exploit simple exaggeration of observed reality and the magical, whether derived from pagan or Christian cultures. Their features are developments of what is found in contemporary reality though formalized and harmonized into the art that is literature.

Arthur's begetting was magical: his father Uther Pendragon, through the magic of Merlin, made love to Igraine in the guise of her husband, the Duke of Cornwall. Then, in the *AMA* and elsewhere, Arthur's heroic and fierce countenance terrifies ambassadors and enemies:

. . .and he looked like a lion, on his lips biting.
The Romans in rank terror cringed on the ground
Through fear of his face as if fated to die.

(AMA)

Something of that idea comes through in the illustration on page 91. In battle, Arthur survives disabling wounds and recovers miraculously to full strength, as indeed does Lancelot, times without number; he slaughters on an impossible scale when making sallies into huge hostile hordes; his strength is such that in the shock of a mounted charge, it is the horse which yields, not the man. In the *AMA*, he twice rises to his knees while dying.

Especially in his most destructive war actions, Nature conspires, beautifying the legitimately gory process with blossoms, flowering trees and pleasant waters which shimmer as they flow. The magical facility which puts the Arthurian hero-king in touch with cosmic supernature in the workings of fate and its ineluctable morality is the capacity to experience prophetic dreams. Very many such dreams are dreamed by fictional Arthurs. The two main dreams of the *AMA*, which are structural in the poem, giving form and meaning to its first and last events, I regard as unrivalled for their force and the poetic quality of their narration. In the first, in his cabin when embarked for France, Arthur dreams of a mighty combat in the sky won by a dragon against a bear, which is interpreted to him as prophetic of his coming victories against the Romans. He dreams the second dream when at the height of his fortunes and about to march on Rome; in it he meets the goddess Fortune, who first pampers him with ravishing delights and then whirls him downwards on her wheel. It is prophetic of his fall.

I hope to have shown that this model medieval king, despite operating under an umbrella of profound social lovingkindness and pious humility, exhibits such qualities as savagery and pride, and a Caliban-like attunement not only to lust, but to the harmonies of Nature. He is at a stage between the primitive and the civilized, and among his virtues displays vices of which our concepts of authority are not yet free. He presents an instructive paradox in the historical development of the human spirit.

VIII PAINTING IN MEDIEVAL ENGLAND

The Wall-to-Wall Message

Pamela Tudor-Craig

And by his side loathsome *Gluttony*,
    Deformed creature, on a filthie swyne,
His belly was up-blowne with luxury,
    And eke with fatnesse swollen were his eyne . . .
(Edmund Spenser, *The Faerie Queene*, 1590)

The Good Man surrounded by roundels of the Acts of Mercy and with inscriptions carrying the names of the theological virtues around him. Trotton, Sussex (c. 1370).

IN SPENSER'S DESCRIPTION, THE SIX DEADLY SINS attendant upon Pride, their sovereign, ride upon the same beasts that were so libelled in the late thirteenth-century moral text, 'the new Mirror of the World', which itself grew out of the French *'Somme le Roi'*. Representations of the seven Deadly Sins mounted upon animals appear in splendid illuminated manuscripts of the fifteenth century, like the English copy of the *Mirror of the World* in the Bodleian Library, or the French book of hours of Jean Dunois, Bastard of Orleans, and in French wall paintings. But we could not be sure that the imagery of Gluttony riding a pig, Lechery a goat, Avarice a camel, Envy a wolf, Sluggishness an ass and Wrath or Pride variously upon a lion, was common medieval currency — until 1985. In that year, the paintings on the south nave wall of St Mary's Hardwick in Cambridgeshire were rediscovered. They had been exposed briefly in 1858, when they had been interpreted as a series of 'messengers riding on different beasts for variety' or 'the legend of Charlemagne's encounter with St Cyriac'. Either way, the then incumbent found them distasteful, and obliterated them again, fortunately by whitewashing over rather than scraping off. In 1985, they were refound at the outset of an intended redecoration scheme, and instantly recognized by David Park for what they are: the seven Deadly Sins riding on their maligned beasts, with the seven Acts of Mercy above them.

106

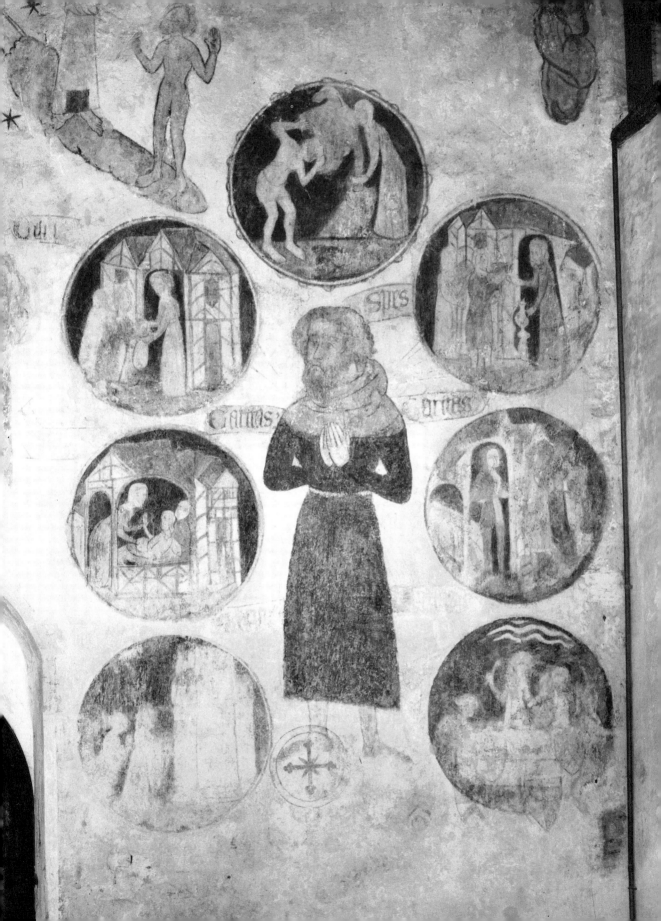

As Spenser drew upon native tradition, so did Shakespeare. The Ages of Man (which in *As You Like It* Jaques describes) were painted around wheels, one of twelve and the other of ten stages, in miniatures of *c.* 1300 in the psalter of Robert de Lisle. More pertinently, the ghost of such a wheel survives on the north-west wall of SS Peter and Paul, Leominster, Herefordshire and at Longthorpe (see below). Shakespeare is unlikely to have studied the theological diagrams of the late thirteenth-century Franciscan John of Metz; to appreciate this imagery the playwright need only have whiled away a sermon by gazing at a wall painting. The survival into the seventeenth century of many wall paintings is suggested by the quantity of imagery left for William Dowsing and his bullies to obliterate during the Civil War.

The wheel form was used in medieval wall paintings for several purposes, latterly the most common being the seven Acts of Mercy. At Hardwick, and at Trotton in Sussex, they are matched with the seven Deadly Sins, a visual and numerical *aide-mémoire* that kept the Divine Counsels of Matthew xxv.35–40, reflected in *The Lyke Wake Dirge*, or the Last Judgement scene of a mystery play, well before the eye. A thirteenth-century wheel of fortune adorns the wall of the choir at Rochester Cathedral — what was its purpose there under the eyes of the religious who had eschewed her guiles? A wheel of fortune was 'realized' in the round for the wedding festivities of Margaret of York and Charles the Bold in 1468. There is a mid-thirteenth-century drawing by Villard de Honnecourt showing a three-dimensional wheel with a little puppet rising and falling with its gyrations, and such 'toys' have been made in our own time. The idea was inherited by the high Middle Ages from Cicero through Boethius's then universally read and admired *Consolation of Philosophy* in which Fortune is described:

> With domineering hand she moves the turning wheel,
> Like currents in a treacherous bay swept to and fro:
> Her ruthless will has just deposed once fearful kings
> While trustless still, from low she lifts a conquered head.

Fickle Fortune lost none of her fascination in the 1,000 years between Boethius and John Skelton, who took up the theme in his *Magnificence*:

> Syr, remember the tourne of Fortune's whele,
> That wantonly can wynke and wynche with her hele.
> Nowe she wyll laughe, forthwith she wyll frowne:
> Sodenly set up and sodenly pluyckyd downe.

108

Another wheel, this time of the senses, forms part of the remarkable series of wall paintings that was discovered through a fall of plaster when, during the last war, a dart missed the board in Longthorpe Tower, near Peterborough. Longthorpe presents the almost complete survival of the decoration of a single modest room in a tower house of perhaps 1330. We could not have guessed how varied such a decoration might be. The Nativity and a series of Apostles are not out of the way, nor are Evangelist symbols or David playing his harp, which adorn the vault. It is interesting to find a set of labours of the months outside a manuscript calendar. There is a scene from the life of St Anthony the Hermit. The encounter between Three Living and Three Dead Kings was a popular *memento mori* from the late thirteenth century.

The most appealing feature at Longthorpe is a range of marshland birds painted on the dado. In 1981 the continuing programme of conservation at Barton Church in Cambridgeshire found a lively group of marginalia, including St Dunstan tweaking the Devil's nose, below the string course along the north nave wall. Barton and Longthorpe, in the second third of the fourteenth century, are contemporary with the amusing and naturalistic margins of East Anglian manuscripts. Like misericords and the borders of illuminated pages, the lower levels of walls were clearly regarded as proper places for topics of less than high theological seriousness. Even more recently, careful exploration of the ruined plaster round the south door at Barton established the scene of St Francis preaching to the birds, of which the earlier representation in England, at Wissington in Suffolk, was painted less than forty years after the saint's death.

About half of the most interesting medieval wall paintings in England have been discovered in the last thirty years. There is no other field of medieval art where the prospects of finding new material of importance are so high. The survey undertaken by David Park of all surviving wall paintings in England has shown that there are at least three times as many as we had previously known, and yet more may come to light every time a church decides to redecorate, or somebody knocks ancient plaster with a broom head. In times past, parishes regarded the discovery of medieval wall paintings with dismay. They foresaw endless expense and much confusion in their churches. However, it is now becoming generally recognized that the possession of wall paintings greatly enhances a building.

Nor is this only a matter for ecclesiastical consideration. The discovery in 1988 that the medieval cottages in Silver Street, Ely, had interesting wall paintings has, in 1990, been crowned by their magnificent conservation and display. One entire wall is covered with a vine-scroll of the fourteenth century, which is comparable with the wonderful fourteenth-century vine-scrolls at Little Witchingham in Norfolk. Perhaps the greatest delight, however, is the discovery in the upstairs room of the easternmost cottage of a series of birds painted, or rather offset in white, against a red ground with floral decoration. Each bird carries a message — the dove has an inscription 'Deale Justlye'; the heron says 'Bear no Malice' and the peacock 'Be not Proud'. In addition to the aptness to their characters as understood partly through Aesop, it is possible that these little phrases have an onomatopoeic reference. One can voice 'Deale Justlye' and 'Be not Proud' in terms of the known cries of those particular birds. There is a parallel in the scrolls carried by the Elizabethan Nativity paintings in Shulbrede Priory in Sussex, where, for example, the duck says 'Quando Quando', the bull 'Ubi Ubi' and the lamb 'in Bethlehem'. The thought that other medieval cottages may yet conceal paintings of this importance and beauty is tantalizing. The famous wall paintings of religious subjects against lush brocade backgrounds in modest rooms of cottage 68, Piccott's End, Hemel Hempstead have provoked speculation about secret gatherings for unorthodox worship. The Silver Street in Ely discoveries, however, lead us to hope that there may be traces of other schemes of similar interest in ancient houses without ecclesiastical connections. Perhaps the first surviving record of the great prayer, 'God be in my head . . .' is the one around a room in Wells in Somerset.

With the help of English Heritage, the problems of those who find that their houses have wall paintings, with all the responsibilities entailed, are beginning to be tackled sympathetically. Nevertheless, like a thatched roof, the possession of wall paintings is both a burden and a distinction for house owners. In the case of churches, many rate English Heritage grants precisely because they have wall paintings. The same should be true of houses. Parish involvement is still heroic — witness the prodigious efforts at fund-raising which have been so successful at Trotton in Sussex.

Trotton has long been famous for its west wall, where a figure of Christ on the rainbow presides over two giant figures of the Good and the Evil Man. From the Evil Man spring the seven Deadly Sins supported by dragons. Around the Good Man cluster the seven Works of Mercy. Over his head is inscribed 'SPES' (hope), at either shoulder is written 'CARITAS' (charity), and the now blank inscriptions either side of his legs no doubt read 'FIDES' (' . . . and *faithfulness* the girdle of his reins', Isaiah xi.5).

By 1984, the condition of the then unexplored north and south nave walls was beginning to cause grave concern. Painstaking struggle established what appeared for months to be almost meaningless areas of red pigment — perhaps a tall figure with a dog — and has now emerged as the most startling series of over life-size military figures in full heraldic panoply. It was known that the west wall of Trotton Church spoke of the new late fourteenth-century vividness of Christian understanding associated with Wyclif's translation of the Bible and with mystical texts like *Piers Plowman*. Now it would seem that the side walls at Trotton provide a statement (personal, genealogical and assertive) of the Camoys family, going beyond the liberal use of heraldry in stained glass, or the creation of the first chantry chapels, as at Cartmel, Cumbria, or in Tewkesbury Abbey, Gloucestershire. No wonder Trotton is contemporary with the first portrait effigies, of which Edward III's (d. 1377) is the English landmark.

Such is the richness of the discovery, and width of implication, social, historical, religious, heraldic, that has emerged from the walls at Trotton through a conjunction of fine craftsmanship and inspired leadership. On a more modest scale, at Troston in Suffolk, a private donation has reinstated the figure of Christ Blessing over the chancel arch. What more eloquent memorial could be devised? Only where there is private funding are conservators at liberty to investigate the entire building, revealing and consolidating everything that survives. Public funds will repair only what is already known. Yet every concealed wall painting risks the tragic destruction that overcame one of the finest of all late fourteenth-century wall paintings at Great Wakering in Essex.

However, more and more often parishes provide hospitality, while the bulk of the funding, which has recently grown significantly, but must still be inadequate, comes from English Heritage with further supplies from the Council for the Care of Churches. In Germany, it is possible to budget for the equivalent of £2 million to be spent over a decade on the total reinstatement of a major medieval interior, with all the ancillary study and recording needed. Only when surviving painted churches are able to rely on similar funding will justice be done to their fascination and utmost delicacy. There are several teams of fine conservators working in the United Kingdom, two of them trained by the legendary Professors Robert and Eve Baker, who did so much to establish this scrupulous and highly professional skill; and a third with its roots in Germany, where, as everywhere on the continent, the care of wall paintings is a generally recognized public duty. Under David Park's aegis, the Courtauld Institute of the University of London is training young conservators in the field. Nothing is lacking but national funding about four times larger than at present.

Should you uncover a corner of a wall painting, resist the temptation to continue the exploration and call in the Council for the Care of Churches at 83 London Wall, EC2. You might have a masterpiece under your hand.

What about Little Witchingham? Who would have expected to find in that deserted Norfolk church, with its roof already fallen in, a cycle of some of the most superb mid-fourteenth-century wall paintings in England? The scheme at Little Witchingham includes a series of Old and New Testament subjects, SS George and Christopher, trails of fine foliage and, in the spandrels of the nave towards the aisle, spectacular roundels of the four Evangelist symbols. Funds did not keep pace with the fragility and urgency of the task: a whole section of the Old Testament paintings on the south wall fell, shattered, to the ground. Even now, the west wall, in a perilous condition, remains unexplored. Churches relatively seldom fall down, but wall paintings collapse only too readily. At Little Witchingham there was a potential clash of conservation interests between fourteenth-century painting and bats nesting in the gaping cavity between plaster and wall.

Symbol of St Matthew: spandrel dating from the first half of the fourteenth century in the south nave arcade at Little Witchingham, Norfolk.

One of the reasons for the acute delicacy of English Gothic wall paintings is that the more stable technique of fresco, the application of colour to the plaster while it is still wet, in patches of one day's work at a time, was abandoned in England about 1200. To true fresco, of course, we owe the

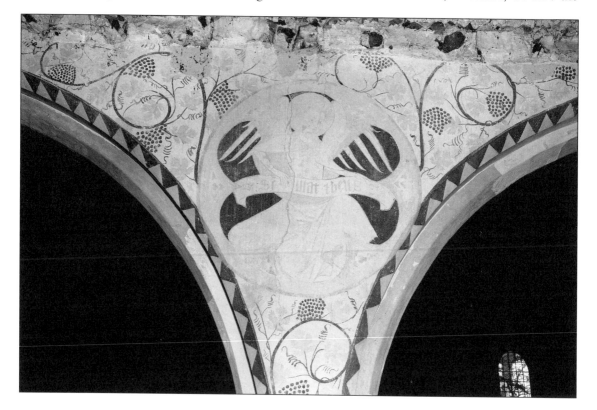

great Romanesque cycles of Kempley, Hardham, Ickleton and Clayton. They may have lost their brilliance, which was in part due to final touches applied after the plaster was dry, but their stability, as part of the texture of the wall itself, has given them a remarkable life span. After 1200 English wall painting was applied by the easier method of working on the dry plaster.

The thinking behind the technical change was not only the temptation to take a short cut. While the craft of fresco is admirably suited to the formalized Byzantinism of the twelfth century, English art in the thirteenth century in all media returned to the more spontaneous affection for the immediate line, which had been the special characteristic of native art before the Norman Conquest. The flowing and urgent linearism of English art — long ago identified by Sir Nicholas Pevsner — is hard to maintain with the rigid mosaic of patchwork demanded by fresco. The first Italian painter who attempted to introduce the full dynamic into wall painting, Leonardo da Vinci, also experimented in alternatives to true fresco. The way in which the fresco technique irons out the vitality of design which mattered so much to English taste can be demonstrated by comparing almost any Italian fresco with the brilliance and pace of the sinopia, the original sketch on the first plaster, beneath it. Artistically speaking, English Gothic wall paintings are much more like tinted sinopie than Italian frescos.

Clearly, our Gothic patrons preferred the immediacy of this effect, which allowed for the subtlety and gentleness, for instance, of the Chichester Roundel, a wall painting of the thirteenth century in the Bishop's Palace Chapel there. Bishop Richard of Chichester (1197–1253), author of the most intimate of medieval prayers ('May I see Thee more clearly, follow Thee more nearly, love Thee more dearly ...'), knew, perhaps commissioned, in his private chapel, this supremely tender image of the loving relationship between Christ and his Mother. It is blemished for us, alas, by the spreading and blackening of the silver with which the angels' censers were painted, but we may still glimpse the vision that inspired St Richard.

The penalty for our choice of the more vital technique is that we cannot expect great areas of Gothic wall painting to survive to a large extent, and few of them do. The chancel at Chalgrove, Berkshire, the naves of West Chiltington, Sussex and Peakirk, Cambridgeshire are among such survivals. Prominent among complete schemes are the two glorious cycles in Winchester Cathedral, the vault paintings of the Guardian Angel's Chapel, and the rendering in two layers, now separated by Mrs Baker, of the cycle of the Entombment and Resurrection, whereby a chapel hollowed out of the north-east crossing pier becomes, like the chapel at Liget near Poitiers, a Holy Sepulchre.

Another complication in the study of Gothic wall paintings is the freedom with which they were repainted. We know from documents that royal patrons were constantly improving their palatial walls. The brilliant paintings in the refectory of the priory at Horsham St Faith's in Norfolk, representing the highest standard of thirteenth-century work, were also updated a century later. One of the puzzles, and rewards, of English wall painting is the frequency with which provincial examples, like Horsham St Faith's, are of incredibly high quality. At Polebrooke in Northamptonshire hardly more than a shadow survives of a series of great figures, painted within the blind arcading of the north transept (a scheme more at home in a Cluniac House of the twelfth century). A humble village church — but real gold gleams from the haloes. Down a farm track in a remote part of Essex, work of a standard worthy of the patronage of Richard II is emerging.

A mid-thirteenth-century roundel of the Virgin and Child in the Bishop's Palace Chapel, Chichester, probably commissioned by Bishop Richard Rich.

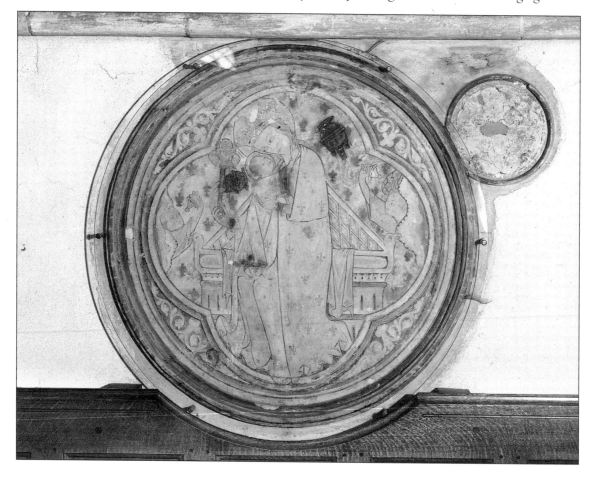

Perhaps the most striking single example of superb work deep in the countryside is the east wall of Brent Eleigh Church in Suffolk. Here, in 1960, Jack Penton visited the church because he knew the decorators were coming in, and was able, by a hair's breadth, to prevent the destruction of what are now three of the most impressive paintings in the country. To the south, a great Harrowing of Hell, with its patron, compares with the two surviving arcade figures, SS Christopher and Doubting Thomas, in the south transept of Westminster Abbey. At the north end of the east wall of Brent Eleigh, the silhouettes of two censing angels flank what was once a real pedestal carrying a figure in three dimensions of the Virgin and Child. In the middle, above the altar itself, the Crucifixion was painted in the early fourteenth century within a simulated frame. The simplicity and eloquence of the three isolated figures, swaying in agony and grief, against a long green ground makes this one of the international masterpieces of the early fourteenth century.

If the twelfth century was the heyday of complete cycles expounding the life of Christ and the doctrine of the Redemption in continuous paintings throughout the church, the thirteenth, and in particular the fourteenth and fifteenth centuries, moved towards a more anecdotal approach to the decoration of our churches. A prime exception, of great interest, is the treatment of the nave at Corby Glen in Lincolnshire. There, in the late fourteenth century, a major scheme of the approach of the kings and of the shepherds to the enthroned Virgin and Child occupies the whole length of the building. The obvious parallel is with the great mosaic schemes of eight centuries before at Sant' Apollinare Nuovo in Ravenna. If Corby Glen's scheme had not survived, we might not have realized that such a processional use of the nave had been carried out in an English church in the late fourteenth century.

It would be easy to suggest that Gothic painting witnesses a steady decline from the majestic schemes of the twelfth century, through the lively free-hand work of the thirteenth century (Great Tew in Oxfordshire, Thornham Parva in Suffolk), the charm of the fourteenth century (South Newington in Oxfordshire, Purton in Wiltshire, the Ante-Reliquary Chapel in Norwich), to brusque peasant work in the fifteenth century (Breage, perhaps, in Cornwall). Even where there is a certain technical coarseness in the later paintings, they have the immediate impact of the mystery plays. At Corby Glen, nervous faces peep from behind the sheltering cloak of a *mater misericordia*. At Nether Wallop, Hampshire, and at Breage, a gigantic wounded Christ is surrounded by the tools of country occupations. The message — that those who continue to work through the Sabbath still wound the body of Christ — could be taken to heart by many workaholics. At Broughton, Buckinghamshire, the Virgin carrying her dead son, the *pietà*, is surrounded by the abuses of riotous living. The language may be more sophisticated when the art is Michelangelo's, but the moral is the same. Even the graph of a general visual decline is an over-simplification. St Gregory's in Norwich, with a fine series of the doctors of the church at the east end of the aisle, in spandrels way above normal eye level, demonstrates the maintenance of high standards after 1400. The west wall of the two aisles at St Gregory's, Norwich, the only non-articulated surfaces in the building, are fields for spectacular pictures by an artist who is a worthy English parallel to the Veronese, Pisanello.

The continuation of good wall painting in the context of the highly panelled lean walls of Perpendicular churches comes as a surprise. Yet the frequent provision in the fourteenth and fifteenth centuries of niches which are too shallow for sculpture argues the intention of filling them with painted figures. This intention was certainly fulfilled at Great Ellington in Norfolk, where a seated Virgin and Child are adored by angels, and in the south-east chapel of Exeter Cathedral. No doubt it was the aim to fill Perpendicular panelling with series of painted figures, in the same way that the tracery of Perpendicular windows, lights large and small, conforms to the shape of the human figure, and provides ranks of niches for their encompassing. If the stained glass figures nowhere survived, we might not realize the implications of Perpendicular window design; so we must allow that the walls were meant to continue the array. Apart from the putative filling of panelling with iconographic schemes, the discovery of painting as fine as that of Eton College Chapel in the Deanery at Durham again proves that there was splendour towards the end of the Middle Ages. Another example has been revealed in the chancel of St Mary le Crypt in Gloucester. As part of their conservation, Madeleine Katkov and Christof Oldenburg have made a reconstruction of the fragmentary remains, showing that major wall paintings of considerable ambition were possible on the eve of the Reformation.

The archaeology of wall paintings is perhaps the most delicate and intriguing of all archaeological disciplines. An ancient wall may have its original twelfth-century frescoed plaster upon it. If only we could treat the east wall of Wareham Church in Dorset appropriately, who knows how many layers of painting we might uncover there? At Willingham in Cambridgeshire there are six layers, running from the thirteenth to the seventeenth centuries. Over the original scheme of grave theological import, the fourteenth and fifteenth centuries overlaid their favourite subjects,

The figure of St Faith (c. 1270) in the refectory of the priory at Horsham St Faith, Norfolk.

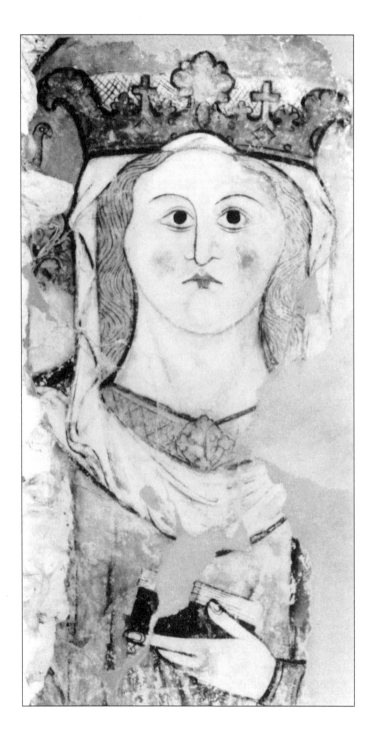

among which martyrs who had endured the most protracted sufferings, shorthand moral schema and images dwelling on the Passion of Christ were specially favoured. Over these again, the Reformation would lay their texts in the vernacular and their royal arms. So the discovery of a few post-Reformation letters of the Lord's Prayer or 'Thou Shalt Not . . .' are enough to tell us that centuries of medieval paintwork may lie beneath.

Had we entered our parish churches in the Gothic centuries, we would have come into a world more like a present Orthodox church than anything we see in the Anglican Communion today. The whole interior surface would have been decorated. The thread of continuity was carried out in the thirteenth century in trefoil masonry patterns with stencilled flowers, or in sprays of foliage, and the subject matter was usually in sustained ribbons of narrative. In the fourteenth century, the foliage became more naturalistic, to develop towards the fifteenth century into luscious brocade patterning. One of the best later examples of the general effect is the chapel at Haddon Hall in Derbyshire.

By the late Middle Ages, the focus had shifted to specific images, obviously commissioned by individuals. Window splays, and areas around doors and windows, had always been favourite positions for special saints or for the Annunciation. If you looked upon St Christopher, you were safe to travel that day, so he is usually placed opposite the main or south door. The chancel arch was given over to a Doom or Last Judgement, awful *caesura* between our earthly life, represented by the nave, and the heavenly life, symbolized by the chancel.

The relative conformity of most churches to these ground rules means that the slightest fragment of a popular subject allows us to deduce the rest: a mermaid or a giant toe indicates St Christopher; one of the dead in a shroud, or the teeth of hell's mouth denotes the Doom. The knowledge and intuition of Mrs Baker was such that she could go to a church like Amberley in Sussex and expose one fourteenth-century head, now looking through a window from a level an inch or two behind the present limewash surface.

Osbert Lancaster's cartoon of 'Professor Isolde's "cleaning" of St George and the Dragon in Drayneflete church' is only partly a joke. Follow 'Professor Isolde's' clues carefully: he had evidence. Nowadays, however, we would not reconstruct a fragmentary wall painting but provide a key to its understanding, probably in the form of a clear drawing.

The abiding fascination of Gothic wall paintings can be illustrated by a morsel in a house at Cley-next-the-Sea in Norfolk. The pedestal of the standing object is of late medieval shape. The object itself has been interpreted as a mirror. The beast is surely a unicorn — note the horn. One of the glorious tapestries of the five senses in the Cluny Museum in Paris illustrates the sense of sight by a unicorn looking into a mirror. Do we have at Cley the footprint of a cycle of the senses?

Wall paintings, however fragmentary, offer a rich field for careful guesswork. It took 130 years to understand Hardwick. One deciphered clue can shed much light on what really mattered to the people of the Middle Ages. We have only a few pieces of the jigsaw that the Puritans tossed to the floor, and they burnt the picture on the lid of the box. Nevertheless, we can often work it out. Wall paintings are the Rosetta Stone of the English Middle Ages.

Why is it that a wall-painted church, even when the design is totally fragmented, of humble execution and of many periods, is always a pleasure to the eye as well as instructive to the mind? One of the reasons lies in a fundamental unity and simplicity of colour. Very seldom is there a wider range than outlines in lamp black, a blocking in earth red and touches of copper green heightened with white.

The frame of medieval paintings is the building: it is a strategic error to attempt to neaten them up by providing artificial borders. We have learned over the whitewashed centuries to read the architectural members, columns, arches and windows, as the positive parts of the design. To the medieval painter they were the negative, the interruptions in the surface that through centuries going back to classical times he had become so skilled at using. Unlike his Victorian reviver, the Gothic painter was not subservient to the building, nor did he cut it up into rectangles as though he were hanging a summer exhibition. The very apertures and angles were pressed into service. He seized long slithers of space for figures of elongated elegance, like the early fourteenth-century Annunciation flanking the west window in Prior Crauden's Chapel at Ely. A range of aisle window splays as at Nassington in Northamptonshire receives a series of courtly saints. In the Chapter House at Westminster Abbey, a central alcove reserved for the abbot is stamped with further authority by being painted with a figure of Christ reigning over the Last Judgement.

The secret Chapel of St Faith in Westminster Abbey is one of the best places to appreciate the power and importance of English Gothic painting. The awe-inspiring and attenuated figure of St Faith stands within a canopy as impossibly slender as Pompeian painted architecture. She broods over a little reredos and a timidly interceding Benedictine monk. Her design reflects the lost sculpted figures from the north portal, as well as the sophistications of the Westminster retable. Reflect upon her mysterious presence — and then try to imagine the wall where she presides scraped to the ashlar . . .

IX WOMEN'S PIETY AND PATRONAGE

Veronica Sekules

Statue of Eleanor of Castile by Alexander of Abingdon from Eleanor Cross at Waltham 1291–2.

THE VAIN LADY MEDE IN WILLIAM LANGLAND'S fourteenth-century poem, *The Vision of Piers Plowman*, is implored by a friar to pay for the glazing of an expensive window, in return for his absolving her sins of licentiousness. Thereby she could have her name inscribed and be certain of Heaven. Certainly, she declared, she would be his friend and never fail him if he continued to have mercy on the frailty of the flesh and forgive those who succumbed to lechery, 'and I shall roof your church, build the cloister, whitewash the walls and glaze the windows and have painted and portrayed she who paid for the works so that everybody shall see that I am sister of your house'. Langland concludes by deploring Lady Mede's vainglory in thus broadcasting her munificence. The story was undoubtedly intended to strike a chord in the reader, for what it describes is an exaggerated version of what we know happened very frequently. The friars do seem to have been especially adept at persuading wealthy and pious women to build or decorate their churches and to provide them generously with alms. For example, the Oxford Blackfriars community was dependent in the 1230s and 1240s for a large part of its existence on the generosity of Isabel de Bolbec, Countess of Oxford, who endowed it with an estate and some meadowland, built decent lodgings for the friars, the cloisters and a 'fair and stately church', earning her the name of foundress. A description of her moral welfare is not recorded and presumably nobody really expected to be absolved of mortal sins like lechery in return for even major benefactions. Attendant on any benefaction was a request for the saying of prayers on the obit (anniversary day of the death) of the donor in order to assist the soul's passage through purgatory. Presumably, it was this custom that Langland was satirizing in *Piers Plowman*.

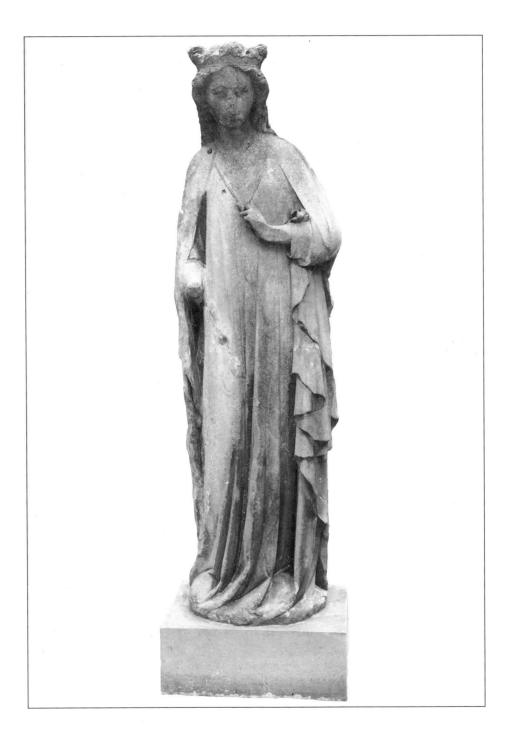

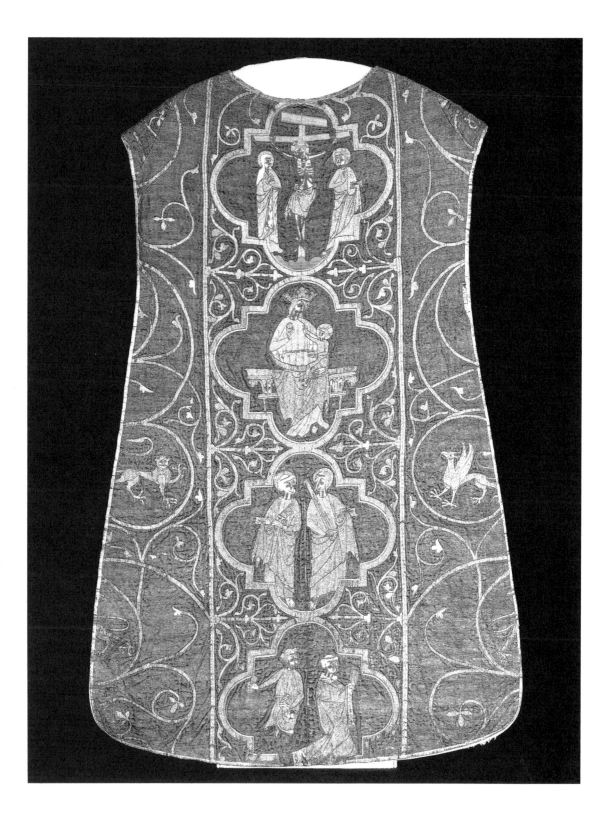

It must be the case that many benefactors were persuaded by the fact that their peers were also contributing. For many years, it was clearly customary for women in fashionable and courtly circles to patronize the friars, and one sometimes finds a kind of kinship group of donors associated with particular foundations. Since they first came to Britain, both the Franciscan and the Dominican friars had been favoured by royalty. Each of the Plantagenet kings had Dominican personal confessors and gave generously to numerous foundations. Their queens shared an affection for the friars. Eleanor of Castile, Edward I's first wife, gave 100 shillings in her will to each of thirty-nine Dominican houses. The Blackfriars of London, in whose friary church the heart of her son Alfonso was buried, received 200 marks and *her* heart too was buried in the choir there in a tomb adorned by images and paintings. The London Greyfriars had an even more illustrious tradition of female royal patronage. The house was founded by Eleanor of Provence, Henry III's queen, and her heart was also buried in the choir. Margaret, Edward I's second wife, was regarded as their second founder, since she paid for a magnificent new church and was in turn buried there. Edward II's queen, Isabella, paid for the completion of the church after 1327, and for the glazing of a window at the east end. She was buried in the choir in 1358 in an alabaster tomb.

Apart from the donations that they made to the Franciscan and Dominican friars, English queens of the thirteenth and fourteenth centuries were not especially generous in their patronage of the arts. Eleanor of Castile is not remembered particularly for any of her own artistic projects, but principally for the remarkable series of memorials to her: the twelve Eleanor crosses, which Edward I commissioned at her death in 1290. Queen Isabella had among her chapel furnishings an alabaster figure of the Virgin and a broken one of St Stephen: these are the only sculptures of hers that have been recorded. She also had a number of embroideries associated with her chapel (cushions worked with monkeys and butterflies), a dorsal of worsted painted with a Nativity and a wall hanging painted with the Apocalypse, as well as some manuscripts (three missals, a breviary, two graduals and a martyrology). None of these has survived, but the collection was no more nor less than one would expect to find in the private chapel of a noble lady of her distinction. Some gifts of works of art are also recorded: she gave a breviary to her friend Marie de St Pol, Countess of Pembroke, and a cope to Pope John XXII. The only known manuscript which was certainly hers is a rather modest psalter, which may have been made to mark the occasion of her wedding in 1308. One of the finest manuscripts of the early fourteenth century, the very lavishly illustrated Queen Mary Psalter,

The Clare Chasuble (pre-1284), probably commissioned by Margaret de Clare.

has also been attributed to her patronage. Unfortunately, this has not been proved, but the choice of illustrations, in which women, particularly biblical queens and noblewomen feature prominently, suggests that it is likely to have been made for a very high-born woman.

Philippa of Hainault does not seem to have been very interested in public works of building or of art or major benefactions. She gave some £48 to the Greyfriars of London and supervised repairs and alterations, mainly of a modest nature, at various castles of which she had custody. At Odiham, she had an enclosed garden made for her own use. She did run up very large debts, however, and her principal extravagance seems to have been clothes. Even after Edward III cleared debts of over £5,000 for her, she was spending £2,000 each year on clothes between 1360 and 1369, which was a phenomenal sum, equal to the cost of all twelve Eleanor crosses. In the light of this extravagance on personal adornment, it is exceptionally interesting that Philippa commissioned her own tomb two years before her death. The white marble effigy by her fellow countryman, Jean de Liège, cost £133. 6s. 8d. and it is the first medieval effigy in England to show a person realistically. Effigies of women were particularly stereotyped in the thirteenth and for most of the fourteenth centuries; there are no female equivalents of the active knights, lying cross-legged or half-rising as if ready for battle. Women were normally shown as if they were standing or lying still, engrossed in prayer, looking youthful and slender. Eleanor of Castile's effigies on the Eleanor crosses set the fashion for the end of the thirteenth century and appearances of female effigies changed only marginally from this type for the next fifty years. Her face has small dainty features, giving no sense of her character, her gently inclining body is voluminously draped in clothing. In complete contrast, Philippa is portrayed with a fleshy ageing face and portly body revealed by a figure-hugging bodice to her dress, and a real sense of an individual personality.

Queen Philippa's tomb was paid for by Edward III and had we only that piece of knowledge, without the circumstantial evidence of her involvement, it would have appeared to have been entirely his commission. Married women had little independent status, and it is normally very hard to guess, even in the case of queens, to what extent they were involved in artistic matters, unless we have an enormous amount of information about their households and tastes. Very often, the only means by which a benefaction is identifiable at all is through heraldry, which creates problems in the case of women. Because the majority were beholden for their status to their fathers and husbands, they were rarely, unless heiresses in their own right, manifested heraldically as separate personalities. Even then, there were instances when the arms they bore could be confused with male members of their families. This was potentially the case with Joanna de Stuteville, who in her widowhood adopted her father's arms unimpaled.

Most benefactions to the Church were connected in some way, either directly or indirectly, with the desire of the patrons to secure a greater chance of salvation when they died. A major source of benefactions to the Church, and a certain way for patrons to ensure that they were prayed for, was the foundation of a perpetual chantry. If they had the means, women were as likely to found perpetual chantries as men. Often a chantry foundation was associated with some building activity. The Cantilupe Chantry at Lincoln Cathedral was founded by Nicholas and Joan Cantilupe in 1345, during their lifetime, for two chaplains to say occasional masses for their souls. In 1358, Joan, now a widow, enlarged the chantry to five chaplains saying masses daily. Shortly afterwards, she provided more assets so that the foundation could be further enlarged. This transaction was completed only after her death, but by 1366 there was a warden and seven chaplains, a substantial chantry house for them to live in and a splendid tomb for the patrons in the cathedral. Chantries in parish churches could be associated with comparatively major building activity. The will of Margerie de Crioll of Irchester, Northamptonshire, dated 1319, provides for five chaplains to celebrate mass for her in her own chapel of St John at Lillingstone and five at the Lady Chapel at Corby which she had built. At the substantial parish church at Newark, on the other hand, the chantry founded in 1330 by Maud Saucemer, as a pair to the one which had been founded by her husband in 1326, was clearly a much more modest affair. These two were among nine chantries founded at Newark between c. 1320 and c. 1360, a period of substantial building at Newark, to which the chantries may collectively have contributed some of the funds.

Widows were in a powerful position economically in that they were able to dispose of their property as they wished upon their death. Women of the nobility who chose to remain widows were often generous to the Church and to other needy institutions. As their first duty upon widowhood, they must often have been in the position of acting as executors for their husbands and thereby choosing their tombs, or at least carrying out instructions left to them. This is probably quite an important area of female patronage, where quite a few more discoveries remain to be made. Two of the most famous tombs of knights of the Gothic period, William Longespée at Salisbury and Aymer de Valence at Westminster Abbey, were probably commissioned by their widows, both of whom were powerful, wealthy and devout women. Marie de St Pol, Countess of Pembroke, Aymer de Valence's widow, was only twenty when he died. She never remarried and became a munificent benefactor, endowing a priory of Franciscan minoresses at her manor of Denny in Cambridgeshire, bequeathing money, jewels and reliquaries to Austin friars, Carmelites, Charterhouses and Cistercians and jewelled crosses to Westminster Abbey and St Paul's Cathedral. She also founded Pembroke College, Cambridge, in 1347. Her own tomb was at Denny, where at her express wish her effigy was represented modestly attired in Franciscan habit.

A contemporary and friend of Marie de St Pol was Elizabeth de Burgh, lady of Clare. She paid for the dormitory chapter house and refectory at Clare Priory. She also favoured the Franciscan minoresses and was buried in their friary at Aldgate. She was generous in the giving of alms, paid for the education of promising young clerks in her household and founded Clare College, Cambridge. Her own household was clearly well equipped; she employed four goldsmiths to care for her jewellery and plate and in her will she bequeathed quantities of plate, vestments, hangings and books. Her family had a long tradition of spectacular benefactions. Her sister, Eleanor de Clare, widow of Hugh Despenser the younger, paid for much of the rebuilding of the east end of Tewkesbury Abbey in the 1320s; their mother, Margaret, probably commissioned the famous Clare Chasuble; and their great-grandmother, Isabella Marshal, gave an enormous quantity of chalices, reliquaries, vestments and books to Tewkesbury Abbey just before her death in 1240.

Some patrons must have played an active part in determining the appearance of the objects or buildings they commissioned, but we rarely have the information to be precise about this. A spandrel relief in the south aisle of the choir at Worcester Cathedral shows a woman instructing a mason, and in a few French manuscripts women are shown in conference with masons who are carving incised tomb slabs or preparing masonry on the site of a building. Generally, however, the relationship between patron and artist has to be inferred by judicious interpretation of whatever evidence is available. At Heckington Church in Lincolnshire, a parish church built largely during the first quarter of the fourteenth century, the principal lay benefactor was probably Isabella de Vesci, second cousin of Edward II and a member of Queen Isabella's household. The incumbent, Richard de Potesgrave, a chaplain to Edward II, paid for the building of the chancel. The church is one of the most lavishly ornamented with sculpture of any date in England. Moreover, its subject matter is consistent with the kind of devotional literature concerned with penance for sins and salvation through the sacrament of Christ, which was becoming current in the early fourteenth century, an example being Robert of

A detail of the effigy of William Longespée (c. 1230). This tomb in Salisbury Cathedral is likely to have been commissioned by his widow, Countess Ela of Salisbury.

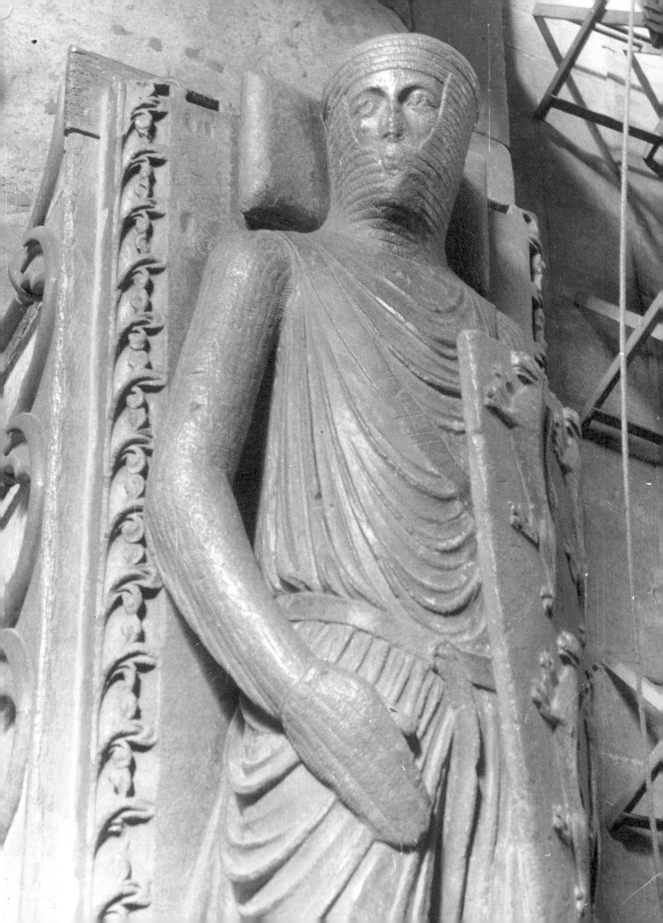

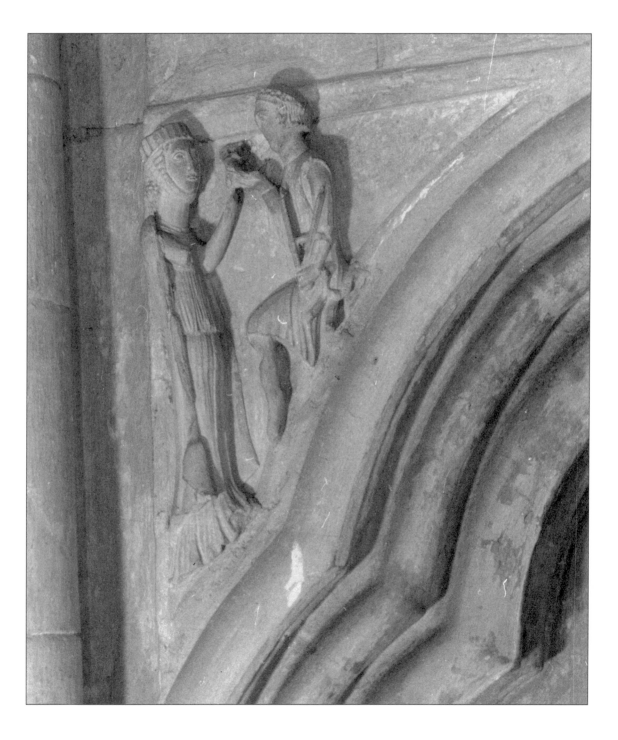

Bourne's *Handlyng Synne* which was written in the immediate locality. Other work by the same masons survives in the region, but in no other case is the imagery so carefully selected, indicating that at Heckington the masons were given firm directions by the benefactors. What is also interesting, given that one of them was a woman, is the range of imagery which is critical of women. Among a large number of corbel sculptures on the exterior are several showing men and women fighting, a number alluding to women's vanity about their appearance and one example of 'Tutivillus and the Gossips', Tutivillus being the devil who sat on the shoulders of women who chattered during the sermon, writing down their words on a long scroll. It is very possible that these images, appearing in the context of a series probably concerned with souls awaiting judgement in purgatory, were deliberately selected to highlight sins peculiar to women, not in order to insult Isabella de Vesci, but out of her humility about the weaknesses of her own sex. From the scant information which survives about how women were instructed in correct and pious behaviour, such as the manual written in the late fourteenth century by the French Knight of la Tour Landry for his three daughters, we learn that genteel women were rigorously drilled in the virtues of obedience, admired for being silent and urged against vanity and extravagant display. What does not survive at Heckington, and which may have redressed the balance in favour of female virtue, are any of the numerous statues of saints which originally would have adorned the exterior.

The more information becomes available about religious works of art commissioned by women, the more it is apparent that many were extremely serious in their devotions and, quite the antithesis of Lady Mede, were constantly striving to be humble and penitent. One little mid-thirteenth-century book of hours in Vienna depicts the female patron three times at prayer. In one illustration, she is kneeling at a prie-dieu with her hair modestly loose; in another, she is kneeling at an altar beholding a vision of Christ holding the host. Another remarkable work of art commissioned by a woman was the Lambeth Apocalypse, a manuscript illustrated with seventy-eight illustrations, which belonged to Lady Eleanor de Quincy, Countess of Winchester, some time in the 1260s. She also seems to have paid close attention to the contents of the manuscript, as it contains a series of special devotional pictures clearly intended for her. One shows a woman armed with the shield of faith, attacked by the devil; the *noli me tangere* shows Mary Magdalene wearing a wimple like Eleanor de Quincy's, as if the noble lady identified with her as the model of a penitent. Her principal identification, however, is with the Virgin Mary; she is depicted wearing heraldic clothing as a supplicant before the Virgin Mary, and there is also a series of images portraying miracles of the Virgin who was the model of

A woman instructing a mason. Spandrel relief in the south choir aisle arcade of Worcester Cathedral (c. 1230).

virtue for women in the Middle Ages. The Knight of la Tour Landry encouraged his daughters to look to the Virgin as an example of obedience, devotion to prayer, modesty, humility, charity, virtuous prudence, courtesy and good nature. Many images survive of female patrons being introduced to the Virgin Mary in a manner which suggests they are looking to her for guidance. In the late fourteenth-century Fitzwarin Psalter, the female donor kneels before the Virgin's mother, St Anne, as she teaches the Virgin to read, as if the donor too is anxious to benefit from the same instruction.

The image of the Virgin being taught to read by her mother first appeared in English manuscripts and panel paintings in the third quarter of the thirteenth century. It is thought that the Dominican friars originated the subject as a means of giving authority to the idea of an education for and by women. There are numerous examples of ecclesiastics, the most famous being Robert Grosseteste, Bishop of Lincoln, who wrote texts specially for their rich female patrons in order to assist them with their household management and education. Although some writings which survive from the period scorn the idea of the necessity for women to read, among the upper classes the ability to read French, at least, must have been widespread. Many devotional texts made for private use by women have glosses or subtitles in French. One psalter made for an English or Scottish noblewoman in the early fourteenth century, the Taymouth Hours, has subtitles in French applying to a curious series of illustrations from romances. Books of romances themselves were often owned by women and Chaucer includes an episode in *Troilus and Criseyde* of women reading romances out loud to each other. For those women who were especially serious about their devotions, knowledge of Latin must also have been advisable. Certainly, Humbert de Romans, general of the Dominicans, wrote that learning was especially important for the daughters of the rich in case they wished to join the religious life or to devote themselves to the study of sacred texts, and to this end he recommended knowledge of the psalter, the Hours of the Virgin, the Office of the Dead and other prayers. Some very learned texts were owned by women. The de Lisle Psalter, given by Lord de Lisle in 1339 to two daughters, contains, as well as the psalter text, a large number of scholarly schematic diagrams including the 'Tower of Theology' of Master John of Metz, the 'Sphera' of John Pecham and the 'Tree of Salvation' of St Bonaventure.

In thirteenth- and fourteenth-century England, women were in a better position to exercise taste in artistic matters as patrons and benefactors than as practitioners. We are not well supplied with information about any artists for the period, but certainly there were some women employed in the various trades. We know that there were female painters, such as Matilda Myms of London, widow of John the 'imaginour', who bequeathed all her own materials to her apprentice William; and Dyonisia La Longe, a gilder, also working in London. These two women also ran alehouses, a common business for women in London. Furthermore, there were female book-binders. In the masons' trade, women either seem to have been allocated menial tasks like mixing plaster or carrying loads, or to have acted as entrepreneurs, running businesses. There are no records referring to any female carvers. The one area of the visual arts in which women practitioners were common was that of textiles. There were many female weavers and embroiderers. One famous name is Mabel of Bury St Edmunds, who worked extensively for the royal court between 1239 and 1245, supplying numerous ecclesiastical vestments and altar furnishings. She both designed and executed her embroideries, as we know from one instance when the king supplied the subjects of SS Mary and John for a banner, leaving the remaining decisions to her.

With their identities generally submerged by those of their fathers and husbands, it is often difficult to be certain about the extent of women's involvement in artistic projects unless they are specifically named. Nearly all art which has survived from the period was connected with the Church, and there was much misogynistic propaganda in clerical writings of the period. Medieval clerics feared the potential that they believed women possessed, as a result of their being descended from Eve, to tempt them away from holiness and chastity. Certainly, this fear was widespread among churchmen and filtered into the public domain; it is manifest in some of the imagery about women, for example among the corbels at Heckington discussed above. Some of the anti-female propaganda, such as the lampooning of the scold and the chatterbox, has persisted to our own day. However, serious female patrons of the arts do not seem to have been deterred by this. The scale of devotion to the religious aspects of their lives, to the churches and the preaching orders they supported is quite remarkable among the pious rich women of the thirteenth and fourteenth centuries. As more research is conducted into the role of women as patrons of the arts in this period, it is increasingly apparent that women played a very much more important role in formulating tastes and setting trends than has hitherto been acknow-ledged.

FURTHER READING

CULTURE AND SOCIETY IN THE AGE OF CHIVALRY

The Cambridge Guide to the Arts in Britain. The Middle Ages, ed. Boris Ford (Cambridge University Press, 1988); *The Age of Chivalry: Art in Plantagenet England 1200–1400*, ed. J. Alexander and P. Binski in the Royal Academy Exhibition Catalogue (Weidenfeld and Nicolson, 1987).

KNIGHTLY CODES AND PIETY

John Harvey, *Gothic England* (Batsford, 1947); R. Barber, *Edward, Prince of Wales and Aquitaine* (Penguin, 1978); Juliet Vale, *Edward III and Chivalry* (Boydell & Brewer, 1982); K. Fowler, *The King's Lieutenant: Henry of Grosmont, 1st Duke of Lancaster* (Paul Elek, 1969); Froissart, *Chronicles*, trans. and ed. G. Brereton (Penguin Classics, 1968); S. Gunn, 'The French Wars of Henry VIII', in *Origins of War in Early Modern Europe*, ed. Jeremy Black (J. Donald, 1987; M. Keen, *Chivalry* (Yale University Press, 1984).

'FORGET-ME-NOTS'
Patronage in Gothic England

English Court Culture in the Later Middle Ages, ed. V.J. Scattergood and J.W. Sherborne (Duckworth, 1983); M. Norris, *Monumental Brasses: the Craft* (Faber, 1978); John Harvey, *The Master Builders* (Faber, 1971); R. Morris, 'Tewkesbury Abbey, the Despenser Mausoleum', trans. *Bristol & Gloucs. Arch. Soc.,* XCIII (1974).

ARTISTS AND CRAFTSMEN

General works on craftsmen are: *English Medieval Industries: Craftsmen, Techniques, Products*, ed. John Blair and Nigel Ramsay (Hambledon Press, 1991), containing a collection of essays on the working methods of different types of craftsmen; Heather Swanson, *Medieval Artisans. An Urban Class in Late Medieval England* (Blackwell, 1989), a socioeconomic survey focused on York;

and John Harvey, *Mediaeval Craftsmen* (Batsford, 1975).

For a medieval account of techniques, one cannot do better than to read Theophilus's treatise, available in two modern translations: Theophilus, *De Diversis Artibus*, ed. C.R. Dodwell (reprinted, Oxford University Press, 1986), and Theophilus, *Of Divers Arts*, trans. John G. Hawthorne and Cyril S. Smith (reprinted with additions, Dover Publications, 1979). The latter version is generally more helpful in interpreting what Theophilus meant.

The craftsmen that have been studied in greatest detail are those of the building trades: see D. Knoop and G.P. Jones, *The Mediaeval Mason* (3rd edn, Manchester University Press, 1967); L.F. Salzman, *Building in England down to 1540: A Documentary History* (reprinted with additions, Oxford University Press, 1967); and John Harvey, *English Mediaeval Architects: A Biographical Dictionary down to 1550* (2nd edn, Alan Sutton, 1984). The achievements of craftsmen who worked for the royal court are set out in *The History of the King's Works*, general ed. H.M. Colvin (HMSO, 1963), volumes I and II. The British Museum's Medieval Craftsmen series of booklets provides well-illustrated accounts of *Embroiderers*, by Kay Staniland; *Glass-Painters*, by Sarah Brown and David O'Connor; *Painters,* by Paul Binski; and *Masons and Sculptors*, by Nicola Coldstream.

THE ARCHITECTURAL SETTING OF GOTHIC ART

The Age of Chivalry: Art in Plantagenet England 1200–1400, ed. J. Alexander and P. Binski in the Royal Academy Exhibition Catalogue (Weidenfeld and Nicolson, 1987); C.N.L. Brooke, *Medieval Church and Society* (Sidgwick and Jackson, 1971); P. Kidson, *The Medieval World* (Paul Hamlyn, 1967); C. Wilson, *The Gothic Cathedral* (Thames and Hudson, 1990); R. Morris, *Cathedrals and Abbeys of England & Wales* (Dent, 1979); C.N.L. and R. Brooke, *Popular Religion in the Middle Ages: Western Europe 1000–1300* (Thames and Hudson, 1984); G.H. Cook, *Medieval Chantries and Chantry Chapels* (John Baker, 1968); G. Dix, *The Shape of the Liturgy* (A. and C. Black, 1945); Durandus of Mende, *The Symbolism of Churches and Church Ornaments*, translation of the first book of the *Rationale Divinorum Officiorum* by J.M. Neale and B. Webb (London, 1843); A. King, *Liturgies of the Past* (Longman Green, 1959); T. Klauser, *A Short History of the Western Liturgy* (Oxford University Press, 1969); H. Kraus, *Gold was the Mortar: the Economics of Cathedral Building* (Routledge and Kegan Paul, 1979); K. Edwards, *The English Secular Cathedrals* (Manchester University Press, 1949); J. Sumption, *Pilgrimage: an Image of Medieval Religion* (Faber, 1975).

DEVOTIONS AND DELIGHTS
The Illuminated Books of Gothic England

M.J. Rickert, *Painting in Britain: the Middle Ages* (2nd edn, Harmondsworth, 1965); Richard Marks and Nigel Morgan, *The Golden Age of English Manuscript Painting, 1200–1500* (Chatto and Windus, 1981); Richard Vaughan, *Matthew Paris* (Cambridge University Press, 1958); Nigel Morgan, *Early Gothic Manuscripts, 1190–1285*, 2 vols. (1982 and 1988) and Lucy Freeman Sandler, *Gothic Manuscripts, 1285–1385*, 2 vols. (1986), both in the series A Survey of Manuscripts Illuminated in the British Isles, ed. J.J.G. Alexander (Harvey Miller); Suzanne Lewis, *The Art of Matthew Paris in the Chronica Majora* (Scolar Press, 1987); Janet Backhouse, *The Luttrell Psalter* (British Library Publications, 1989); Janet Backhouse and Christopher de Hamel, *The Becket Leaves* (British Library Publications, 1988); *The Holkham Bible Picture Book*, ed. W.O. Hassall (The Dropmore Press, 1954).

MEDIEVAL KINGSHIP
Arthur in English Romance

King Arthur's Death: Morte Arthure and Le Morte Arthur trans. and intro. Brian Stone (Penguin, 1988); Sir Thomas Malory, *Le Morte D'Arthur* (Dent, 1906, reprinted 1978); Sir Thomas Malory, *Works*, ed. and intro. Eugene Vinaver (Oxford University Press, 1967); *La Mort le Roi Artu*, ed. Jean Frappier (Droz, 1964); Maurice Keen, *Chivalry* (Yale University Press, 1984); Michael Prestwich, *The Three Edwards* (Methuen, 1981); Christopher Allmand, *The Hundred Years War* (Cambridge University Press, 1988); May McKisack, *The Fourteenth Century*, volume V in the *Oxford History of England* (Oxford University Press, 1959); Stephen Turnbull, *The Book of the Medieval Knight* (Guild Publishing, 1985).

PAINTING IN MEDIEVAL ENGLAND
The Wall-to-Wall Message

David Park's forthcoming book on English wall paintings, published by the Royal Commission on Historical Monuments; Alan Caiger-Smith, *English Medieval Wallpaintings* (Oxford University Press, 1936); E.W. Tristram, *English Medieval Wall Paintings: The Thirteenth Century* (Oxford University Press, 1950); E.W. Tristram, *The Fourteenth Century* (Oxford University Press, 1954); E.

Clive Rouse, *Discovering Wall Paintings* (Shire Publications, 1968, reissued 1983); J.L. Carr, *A Month in the Country* (Penguin, 1980); 'Medieval wall paintings, Silver Street, Ely: a Chronicle', written by members of the Conservation of Wall Paintings Department, Courtauld Institute of Art, University of London (Cambridgeshire Cottage Improvement Society, 1990).

WOMEN'S PIETY AND PATRONAGE

Eileen Power, *Medieval Women*, ed. M.M. Postan (Cambridge University Press, 1975); Margaret Wade Labarge, *Women in Medieval Life* (Hamish Hamilton, 1986); W.A. Hinnebusch, *The Early English Friars Preachers* (Institutum Historicum Praedicatorum, Romae ad Santa Sabinae, 1951); J. Moorman, *A History of the Franciscan Order from its Origins to the Year 1517* (Oxford University Press, 1968); N.J. Morgan, *Early Gothic Manuscripts*, 2 vols. (Harvey Miller, 1988); William Langland, *The Vision of Piers Plowman*, ed. A.V.C. Schmidt (Dent, 1978); *The Age of Chivalry: Art in Plantagenet England 1200–1400*, ed. J. Alexander and P. Binski, in the Royal Academy Exhibition Catalogue (Weidenfeld and Nicolson, 1987); J.J.G. Alexander, 'Painting and Manuscript Illumination for Royal Patrons in the Later Middle Ages' in *English Court Culture in the Later Middle Ages*, ed. V.J. Scattergood and J.W. Sherborne (Duckworth, 1983 pp. 141–62); Thomas Tolley, 'Eleanor of Castile and the "Spanish" Style in England' in *England in the Thirteenth Century* (Proceedings of the 1989 Harlaxton Symposium), ed. W.M. Ormrod (Stamford, 1991); *Eleanor of Castile 1290–1990: Essays to Commemorate the 700th Anniversary of her Death: 28 November 1290*, ed. D. Parsons (Paul Watkins, 1991).

LIST OF CONTRIBUTORS

Nigel Saul is Reader in Medieval History at Royal Holloway and Bedford New College, University of London. He is author of *Scenes From Provincial Life. Knightly Families in Sussex 1280–1400* (1986). Currently he is writing a biography of King Richard II.

Juliet Vale is the author of *Edward III and Chivalry* (1982). She has translated a number of French books on the Middle Ages, most recently *France in the Middle Ages, 987–1460* by Georges Duby (1991).

Malcolm Vale is Fellow and Tutor in Medieval History at St John's College, Oxford. His books include *War and Chivalry* (1981) and *The Angevin Legacy and the Hundred Years War* (1990).

Nigel Ramsay is a curator in the Department of Manuscripts at the British Library. He is the editor of *English Medieval Industries: Craftsmen, Techniques, Products* (1991) and of *St Dunstan: His Life, Times and Cult* (1992).

Peter Draper is Lecturer in the History of Art and Chairman of the Department, Birkbeck College, University of London. He is the Honorary Editor of *Architectural History*, the Journal of the Society of Architectural Historians of Great Britain and was Honorary Editor of the British Archaeological Association Conference Transactions. His publications include 'Architecture and Liturgy' in *The Age of Chivalry*, The Royal Academy Exhibition Catalogue (1987), as well as articles on medieval architecture in various scholarly journals. He is currently writing a book on the transition from Romanesque to Gothic in Britain.

Janet Backhouse is Curator of Illuminated Manuscripts at the British Library. Her publications include *The Lindisfarne Gospels* (1981) and *The Bedford Hours* (1990).

Brian Stone was a founder member of the Open University as Reader in Literature. He is the author of several books, including verse translations and introductions to *Sir Gawain and the Green Knight* (1959) and *The Owl and the Nightingale, Cleanness, St Erkenwald* (1971).

Pamela Tudor-Craig is a medieval art historian. She is Professor of Art History to Grinnell College in London (et al.), Vice-Chairman of the Paintings Committee, Council for the Care of Churches, and a member of the Fabric Committees of Westminster Abbey, Peterborough and Southwell Cathedrals. She is co-author of the Bells Cathedral Guide to Westminster Abbey (1986); *Richard III* (catalogue of her exhibition at the National Portrait Gallery, 1973); and co-author with Richard Foster of *The Secret Life of Paintings* (the book of her TV Series, 1986).

Veronica Sekules is a curator at the Sainsbury Centre for Visual Arts, University of East Anglia. She is author of a number of articles on patronage, on women and the arts and on sculpture and liturgical furnishings in medieval buildings. She is writing a book about women's artistic patronage in the Middle Ages in Europe.

ILLUSTRATION ACKNOWLEDGEMENTS

COLOUR PLATES

Figures refer to plate numbers

1 by permission of the British Library (Weidenfeld Archives); 2 by courtesy of the Trustees, The National Gallery, London; 3 Archbishop of Canterbury and the Trustees of Lambeth Palace Library; 4 Pierpont Morgan Library, New York; 5 by permission of the British Library; 6 Bibliothèque Nationale, Paris; 7 Master and Fellows, Magdalene College, Cambridge; 8 Bodleian Library, Oxford; 9 by permission of the British Library; 10 The Board of Trinity College, Dublin; 11 Susan Haskins; 12 Veronica Sekules; 13 Royal Commission on the Historical Monuments of England (National Survey of Medieval Wall-Paintings); 14 Trinity College, Cambridge; 15 by permission of the British Library; 16 Royal Commission on the Historical Monuments of England (National Survey of Medieval Wall-Paintings).

BLACK AND WHITE ILLUSTRATIONS

Figures refer to page numbers

By permission of the British Library frontispiece; A. F. Kersting 9, 11; Royal Commission on the Historical Monuments of England 14; A. F. Kersting 17, 22, 25; by courtesy of the Trustees of the British Museum 26; Christ Church, Oxford (Weidenfeld Archives) 28; Vicar, Churchwardens and Parochial Church Council of Tewkesbury Abbey 31; A. F. Kersting 33, 37; Royal Commission on the Historical Monuments of England 38; Sydney W. Newbury (Weidenfeld Archives) 39; by permission of the British Library (Weidenfeld Archives) 42; Merton College, Oxford 46; by courtesy of the Conway Library, Courtauld Institute of Art 49; A. F. Kersting 50; by permission of the British Library 53; A. F. Kersting 61; Department of the Environment (Weidenfeld Archives) 63; by courtesy of the Conway Library, Courtauld Institute of Art 66; Aerofilms 70; Howard C. Moore (Woodmansterne Ltd) 72; by permission of the British Library 77; Cambridge University Library 80; by permission of the British Library 84; by courtesy of the Dean and Chapter of Westminster 86; by permission of the British Library 89; Cloisters Museum, Metropolitan Museum of Art, New York 91; Mansell Collection 92; Great Hall, Winchester 95; by courtesy of the Trustees of the British Museum 98; Royal Commission on the Historical Monuments of England (National Survey of Medieval Wall-Paintings) 107, 112, 114, 117; by courtesy of the Board of Trustees of the Victoria & Albert Museum 121, 122; by courtesy of the Conway Library, Courtauld Institute of Art 128.

Frontispiece and photographs on pages 31, 46, 72, 77, 80, 84, 89, 91, 95, 117, 127 and colour plates numbers 4, 5, 7, 9 and 14 supplied by *History Today* Archives.

INDEX to *Age of Chivalry*

Numbers in **bold** refer to colour plates; numbers in *italics* refer to page
numbers for black and white illustration captions